CHRISTIAN ECONOMICS

In One Lesson

Gary North

AMERICAN VISION PRESS
POWDER SPRINGS, GEORGIA

Christian Economics in One Lesson
by Gary North

© Copyright 2016, American Vision, Inc.

Published by:
American Vision, Inc.
P.O. Box 611
Braselton, GA 30517
www.AmericanVision.org

Printed in the United States of America.

ISBN: 978–0–9972402–1–4

This book is dedicated to

Robert Anderson

My successor at FEE in 1973,
who then carried the burden.

Contents

Preface xiii

Introduction. 1

1: The Lesson 13

2: The Broken Window 19

3: The Blessings of Destruction 31

4: Public Works Mean Taxes 39

5: Taxes Discourage Production 49

6: Credit Diverts Production 60

7: The Curse of Machinery 69

8: Spread-the-Work Schemes 77

9: Disbanding Troops and Bureaucrats . . . 85

10: The Fetish of Full Employment 94

11: Who's "Protected" by Tariffs? 104

12: The Drive for Exports 112

13: "Parity" Profits. 119

14: Saving the X Industry 130

15: How the Price System Works 138

16: "Stabilizing" Commodities 150

17: Government Price-Fixing 160

18: Minimum-Wage Laws 166

19: Do Unions Really Raise Wages?. . . . 173

20: "Enough to Buy Back the Product" . . . 183

21: The Function of Profits 193

22: The Mirage of Inflation 200

23: Assault on Saving 210

24: The Lesson Restated 222

Conclusion 232

Appendix:
Henry Hazlitt's Enormous Contribution 239

Preface

You have probably heard of Henry Hazlitt's book, *Economics in One Lesson*.

In 1971, when I was director of seminars for the Foundation for Economic Education, we had a policy of sending out three free books before each week-long seminar: *Clichés of Socialism*, Henry Grady Weaver's *The Mainspring of Human Progress*, and *Economics in One Lesson*.

I do not think it is an exaggeration to say that this book, more than any other, has served as the single most important book in the revival of free-market economic thinking after World War II. Among economists, F. A. Hayek's *The Road to Serfdom* (1944) has been more important, but with respect to the average man, who has probably never read Hayek's book, *Economics in One Lesson* has been the touchstone.

He analyzed the various government interventions in the market by means of the analogy known as "the broken window fallacy," which is also known as "the things seen and the things not seen." The things not seen are the economic costs of the things seen: **the most valuable uses for the money foregone**. This analogy had been devised in 1850 by the French journalist Frédéric Bastiat. This was Hazlitt's one lesson in economics. This was the heart of Hazlitt's book, and it worked in terms of economic analysis. Readers could follow its logic.

The Mises Institute bought the rights to make it available free of charge to anyone who wants to read it. You can download it here: http://mises.org/library/economics-one-lesson.

1. Hazlitt's Audience

When you think about when he wrote it, it is remarkable that he was able to write it. It is even more remarkable that it has sold as well as it has. He was given a six-week leave of absence by *The New York Times* in February 1946. At the time, he was the chief financial columnist for the newspaper.

World War II had ended the previous August. President Truman had not yet removed wartime price and wage controls. He did that only under the pressure of what was basically a revolt by cattlemen the following October. In October, he abolished the price controls on meat. In November, he abolished price controls on wages and most commodities. The only controls remaining after November were on sugar, rice, and rents.

When Hazlitt wrote the book, residents of the United States had been living under price controls for five years. Shortages were a way of life. Rationing had been enforced the entire period. The black market had flourished. So, Hazlitt included a chapter on price controls.

Market by market, intervention by intervention, "broken window by broken window," Hazlitt wrote the book. It has 24 chapters. He did this in six weeks. It was a major accomplishment. Given the enormous impact of the book, it was a startling accomplishment.

But there is a major problem with the book, and this problem keeps getting worse. It is dated. It was written in 1946. He wrote it for a particular audience, and that audience was still living under the economic controls of World War II. The issues that were prominent in the minds of his intended audience were not the same issues that are in the minds of voters today in the United States. Time marches on.

The second problem with the book is this: Ludwig von Mises had not yet written *Human Action*. That book was published in 1949. Hazlitt was a friend of Mises. Mises had arrived in New York City in 1940, a refugee who had fled the Nazis. Hazlitt had read *Socialism* and *The Theory of Money and Cred-*

it. These books had been published in Great Britain before World War II. He had read *Omnipotent Government* and *Bureaucracy*, both published in 1944 by Yale University Press. But Mises' masterpiece was still in the future.

There was a third problem. His audience was made up of literate people who had read his columns for years in *The New York Times*. He was also writing for businessmen. But he was not writing for people in the pews of America's churches. Yet, from the point of view of the size of the audience, he missed a great opportunity. From the point of view of persuading a majority of Americans that government intervention in the marketplace is a bad idea, he had nothing to say. He did not appreciate the size of that audience, and he also had no familiarity with its terminology. He had been a protégé of H. L. Mencken, who was America's most prominent skeptic in the world of the intelligentsia. Mencken had chosen Hazlitt to replace him as the editor of *The American Mercury* in 1933. Mencken was a self-conscious disciple of Frederick Nietzsche. This is not good training for someone writing a book to persuade a majority of America's voters.

Today, every one of the chapters in his book is still applicable in the United States. All of the interventions still exist. Some of them have faded in influence, such as the trade union movement, but all of them still have federal bureaucracies that interfere with the free market. His book did not persuade the masses to elect congressmen and senators, not to mention presidents, who were committed to rolling back the Keynesian administrative state. Things are a lot better than they were in 1946—outside of banking, anyway—but not because of Hazlitt's book. Things began to get better in the fall of 1946, because there were political pressures on Truman to abolish the controls.

It is one of those curious facts that Richard Nixon got his start in Washington during World War II as a bureaucrat with the Office of Price Administration. So did the leftist economist, John Kenneth Galbraith. It was also Nixon who, on August 15, 1971, unilaterally imposed a comprehensive system of price and wage controls on the American economy. He did it by executive order. Those controls created major economic disruptions, and they were abandoned in 1973. But it is clear that Nixon never figured out the truths presented in Hazlitt's book. He did not get over his faith in price and wage controls until first-hand experience persuaded him that they were a bad idea. No book persuaded him of this.

2. A New Audience

I have decided that it is time for me to write a book that I have thought about since 1970: *Christian Economics in One Lesson*. I am going to take each of Hazlitt's chapters, and I'm going to rewrite them in terms of a fundamental Christian principle: thou shalt not steal.

Hazlitt never identified the government interventions that he describes for what they really are, namely, theft. Hazlitt carefully avoided the fundamental ethical issue. He did not raise the ethical question of who, exactly, had broken that famous window, and why. He analyzed what would happen after the window was broken, meaning after the government had intervened in the economy on behalf of some special interest group. Hazlitt identified these groups, and he also identified what their motivation was: to feather their nests. But he did not straightforwardly identify the ethical impulse behind the breaking of two-dozen windows. That was a strategic mistake.

Here is a key problem. Hazlitt knew, as any instructor of freshman economics students knows, that most people cannot handle long chains of reasoning. They can barely handle short chains of reasoning. Hazlitt used the fallacy of the broken window in order to help readers follow a relatively short chain of reasoning. That was as much as he could expect to accomplish. The book achieved this.

There is a secondary problem even with short chains of reasoning. They may persuade minds, but they do not mobilize the troops. People only rarely re-think their lives, and then re-dedicate their lives, on the basis of a short chain of reasoning. The immediate benefits of re-thinking your pre-suppositions are minimal, and the costs are high. If people really do act in terms of their personal self-interest, as economists argue, then only a few of them are going to re-struc-ture their lives on the basis of the application of the analogy of a broken window.

If, on the other hand, you can persuade the person that he has become an accessory, or even an active participant, in breaking somebody else's window, you may be able to gain his attention. You may be able to motivate him by a careful consideration of this principle: thou shalt not steal. If you move the discussion from economic analysis to ethical analysis, you up the ante dramatically. If you move the discussion from a consideration of Adam Smith's invisible hand to an invisible God with a rod of iron, you are more likely to catch people's attention. Anyway, you are more likely to catch the attention of millions of people who spend Sunday morning sitting in the pew.

3. The Social Gospel

Beginning in the 1880's, a movement known as the social gospel began to have influence in the United States. This move-ment was developed by liberal theologians who had adopted welfare state economics. In the name of Jesus and Christian-ity, they came before educated Christians and pastors, per-suading them to adopt welfare state principles and policies in the name of the Bible. This movement became a major intel-lectual force in the mainline denominations after World War I. Some variant of the social gospel still is dominant in all of the mainline Protestant denominations. In the form known as liberation theology, it is dominant in the Roman Catholic Church. The present Pope is a liberation theologian. It was a powerful influence in his life as a young Argentinian.

The social gospel movement did not appeal to Southern Baptists, fundamentalists, and most adherents of what has become known after World War II as the new evangelicalism.

But there have been promoters of the social gospel, which is in fact a statist gospel, within the camp of the evangelicals. The most prominent one today is Jim Wallis. I have a document refuting Wallis on GaryNorth.com.

In the late 1970's, the most prominent figure was Ronald Sider, who wrote *Rich Christians in an Age of Hunger* (1977). I hired David Chilton in 1980 to write a refutation. I believe his book is the most rhetorically powerful response to the social gospel ever written: *Productive Christians in an Age of Guilt-Manipulators*. (I provided the money and the title.) You can download it here: www.bit.ly/chilton-sider.

In the 1990's, the most influential figure was Tony Campolo, a professor of sociology. He lost influence after the Monica Lewinsky scandal broke in 1998, because he had been a spiritual advisor to Bill Clinton. He still serves in this capacity. He says this: "To pastor one great leader in America at a time is enough for any person." I am not making this up. He still has an audience. He gives 200 speeches a year at age 79. He says he plans to write a book on Christianity and the social sciences. I hope he does. It will make a wonderful target.

4. Beating Something with Nothing

I have understood this political principle for all of my adult life: "You can't beat something with nothing."

Free market economists have attempted to overcome the influence of welfare state economics by means of careful discussions of the economic inefficiency of welfare state economics. But people who are profiting from welfare state economics are not impressed. They believe that they come to the voters from an elevated position. They believe that they occupy the moral high ground.

Free-market economists assume that economics is value-free. They never come in the name of the moral high ground, because they believe that, in economic affairs, there is no moral high ground. There is no morality at all. They see the economic public square as a playing field having to do only with personal liberty and economic efficiency. Because of this, they have lost the case. Most people don't vote in terms of economic efficiency. They may vote in terms of personal liberty, but only in those cases in which somebody else has persuaded the government to invade to their personal liberty. They vote to defend themselves from tyranny. Then they turn around and vote to impose tyranny on someone else. They do this in the name of the moral high ground.

What we need is a systematic economic approach that persuades people in the pews that the adoption of welfare state principles and policies is a violation of the commandment not to steal. It is crucial that those people who favor the free market are in a position to persuade those who occupy the pews that the latter's commitment to welfare state policies, Keynesian redistribution policies, and special interest legislation is a violation of the commandment not to steal. This is what Mises refused to do, Hayek refused to do, Friedman refused to do, and, sadly, Hazlitt refused to do.

I decided to do it. I have a tremendous advantage. I read Hazlitt's book and *Human Action* by the time I was 21. I also read Rothbard's *Man, Economy, and State* (1962). That was in 1963. I had a head start on Hazlitt, because Hazlitt had done his work in 1946. The old line about standing on the shoulders of giants is accurate.

The average man in the pew has never heard of Hazlitt, Mises, or Rothbard. But he has heard this: "Thou shalt not steal." This is where I start. Along the way, I take readers on a tour of two-dozen broken windows. After this, I will encourage readers to stop voting for politicians who throw stones at windows in the name of justice and the high moral ground.

Support materials for can be found in the "Further Reading" section at the end of each chapter, where applicable.

Further Reading

For support materials go to bit.ly/CEIOL-Doc-Preface.

Introduction

*C*hristian Economics in One Lesson* is my reworking of
Henry Hazlitt's classic introduction to economic thought,
Economics in One Lesson. That book set the standard as an
introductory economics book. Nothing has come close to replacing it ever since it was first published in 1946.

Why do I believe it is necessary to replace a classic? There
are several reasons. First and foremost, it was written in 1946.
A lot has happened since then, including the publication of
Ludwig von Mises' *Human Action* (1949). Second, it was written under a strict deadline. Hazlitt had been given a six-week
leave of absence, and he had to produce the book from start
to finish. It is possible to do this. I have written several books
in less than a month. I wrote my introductory book on Christian economics, *Inherit the Earth* (1987), in two weeks. But I
had a tremendous advantage at the time, which a year earlier I
would not have enjoyed. I had a structure, as I explain below.
Hazlitt did not have a comparable structure. This made his
work more difficult, and it made the book less effective than it
might have been. Third, he targeted a different audience: readers of his business columns. I target Christians. (Orthodox
Jews are invited to come along for the ride.) Fourth, I place
ethics at the heart of my analysis: the deliberate breaking of
the window. Hazlitt did not—not explicitly, anyway.

1. The Broken Window

He began the book with a classic analogy: Frédéric Bastiat's
broken window. It was a powerful analytical tool when it was

first published in 1850, the year the author died. It was long ignored by professional economists, probably because Bastiat was perceived by them as a journalist at best. Everyone knew that he was a gifted essayist and a master of rhetoric—the art of persuasion. But his essays were never accepted by writers in the field of what was then called political economy. By the time that economics developed as a separate academic field after 1900, he was forgotten.

Then came Hazlitt's book. Hazlitt resurrected Bastiat's brilliant analogy, and then he applied it, chapter by chapter, state intervention by state intervention. He demonstrated the analytical power of the original observation. The fundamental insight of Bastiat was this: the typical observer of economic affairs is blinded by the visibility of the effects of spending. He does not think to investigate what else could have been done with the money. This insight has become the most common definition of economic cost: the most valuable use forgone because a buyer spends the money on something else. Anyone who wants to demonstrate economic logic can do no better than to invoke the broken window analogy.

Every economic decision is something of a broken window. It is the substitution of a new set of conditions for an older set of conditions. Maybe we do not break the old window, but we exchange it for something we think will be better. We come to forks in the road, decision by decision. Once we take a particular fork in the road, we can never return to exactly the same fork. Our world changes at the margin. It changes because of the decision which we made. So, when we think of the cost of any decision, we should always think of it as a decision to go down one road rather than another. We spend our money and we spend our time on one thing, and therefore we cannot spend it on another.

Because public works were popular in France in 1850, and everywhere else, Bastiat's observation helped make it possible to come to grips with the real costs that are borne by individuals and societies when violence is used against a property owner. Just because the government is the violator, this in no way changes the economic analysis of the replacement costs of the broken window.

The power of the analogy is simple, for this reason: we can understand it. It does not involve a long chain of reasoning. We find it difficult to follow long chains of reasoning, and economic analysis, more than any other social science, usually involves long chains of reasoning. People get lost along the way. Also, as the reasoning becomes more complex, people's commitment to the details of the chain of reasoning grows weaker. If it is necessary to argue a point in such a way that not a single link in the chain is left out or misapplied, then the outcome of the chain of reasoning is not clear, either to the person making the argument, or to the person who is listening carefully—initially—and attempting to follow it. *The longer the argument, the less its persuasive strength.* People get bogged down in the details. They cannot keep the details straight. If you can't keep the details straight, you cannot be confident that you have gone from point A to point Z in a systematic and accurate way.

Making effective use of the analogy of the broken window involves pointing to only a couple of short chains of reasoning. There are more chains, and they can be long, but you don't need to follow all of them in order to make your point. Most people can follow this chain, and one of the reasons why they can follow it is the simplicity of the analogy. We can understand a broken window. We can understand the economic burden of replacing that window. We do not get bogged down in a long chain of reasoning.

This is why Hazlitt's book was a success. Bastiat did not make it work in his lifetime. He died in the year he came up with it. A century later, Henry Hazlitt made it work.

My book is not an attempt to reinvent the wheel. My book is an attempt to re-balance the wheel, stick a new tire on it, and to sell it to a new audience.

2. I Begin With Ownership

I believe that Christian economics must begin with the issue of ultimate ownership. This sets it apart from modern economic analysis, which begins with the issue of scarcity. Second, this leads to the issue of theft, which in turn raises the issue of ethics.

I believe that the ultimate form of causation in human history is ethical: right vs. wrong. Modern economists do not share my view. It goes beyond this. They openly reject it. They proclaim economic analysis as value-free. I regard this as self-deception. It is a variation of an ancient temptation: "Hath God said?" Yes, He has. "Thou shalt not steal." There are negative sanctions attached to this commandment. These negative sanctions are both endogenous (inherent in the economy) and exogenous (imposed by God on the economy).

A. Adam Smith's Strategic Error

I come now to a crucial point. I am not the first person to make this point; Tom Bethell is. He did this in Chapter 7 of his book, *The Noblest Triumph* (1998). Adam Smith began with scarcity as the heart of his economic analysis: the famous third chapter in *The Wealth of Nations* (1776). This was on the division of labor/specialization. He set the pattern for subsequent economic theorists.

Smith should have started with ownership. He should have made private ownership the bedrock foundation of his analysis.

By beginning with the division of labor, he committed a strategic error. Critics from the Left immediately challenged him. They were also able to invoke the division of labor. They invoked state planning as a way to deal with the problems of coordinating the division of labor.

The fundamental economic issue, ownership, did not become a major focus of economic theory until the 1950's. So, for almost two centuries, the crucial economic issue had not been central in free market economic analysis.

B. Bastiat's Two Essays

In 1850, the year of his death, Bastiat wrote a long essay, "That Which is Seen, and That Which is Not Seen." In it, he offered an analogy: the broken window. Someone throws a stone through another man's window. That man must now replace his window. He will have to hire a window repairman, who in turn will have to hire others. The broken window has therefore led to greater spending. The economy benefits.

Yet the victim experienced a loss. How can good come out of bad? How can a destructive act produce wealth? This was a paradox that confronted Bastiat. He solved it brilliantly. The owner of the window had other uses for his money. These he regarded as better uses. He either would have saved his money or else he would have spent it on other things besides a new window. In either case, the economy would have benefitted. Other producers would have benefitted. This, he said, is that which is not seen. The spending on the new window is what people see.

In short, he said, "follow the money." Follow the money backwards: back to what he would have done, had not an envy-driven person tossed a stone through that window.

This is a strategy of economic analysis. Bastiat ended his essay by quoting a French author.

> I might subject a host of other questions to the same test; but I shrink from the monotony of a constantly uniform demonstration, and I conclude by applying to political economy what Chateaubriand says of history:—
>
>> "There are," he says, "two consequences in history; an immediate one, which is instantly recognized, and one in the distance, which is not at first perceived. These consequences often contradict each other; the former are the results

of our own limited wisdom, the latter, those of
that wisdom which endures. The providential
event appears after the human event. God rises
up behind men. Deny, if you will, the supreme
counsel; disown its action; dispute about words;
designate, by the term, force of circumstances,
or reason, what the vulgar call Providence; but
look to the end of an accomplished fact, and you
will see that it has always produced the contrary
of what was expected from it, if it was not established at first upon morality and justice" (Cha-
teaubriand's Posthumous Memoirs).

There is a second fact, even more crucial to my book, but
not for Hazlitt's: the issue of ethics. Bastiat wrote another essay in 1850: *The Law*. In that essay, he turned to ethics, namely, the issue of theft. He described the welfare state. He also
identified its underlying motive. He called this *the politics of
plunder*. He wrote:

The Fatal Idea of Legal Plunder

But on the other hand, imagine that this fatal principle has been introduced: Under the pretense of organization, regulation, protection, or encouragement,
the law takes property from one person and gives it
to another; the law takes the wealth of all and gives it
to a few—whether farmers, manufacturers, ship owners, artists, or comedians. Under these circumstances,
then certainly every class will aspire to grasp the law,
and logically so.

The excluded classes will furiously demand their right
to vote—and will overthrow society rather than not to
obtain it. Even beggars and vagabonds will then prove
to you that they also have an incontestable title to vote.
They will say to you:

"We cannot buy wine, tobacco, or salt without paying the tax. And a part of the tax that we pay is given
by law—in privileges and subsidies—to men who are
richer than we are. Others use the law to raise the prices of bread, meat, iron, or cloth. Thus, since everyone
else uses the law for his own profit, we also would like
to use the law for our own profit. We demand from the
law the *right to relief*, which is the poor man's plunder.
To obtain this right, we also should be voters and legislators in order that we may organize Beggary on a
grand scale for our own class, as you have organized
Protection on a grand scale for your class. Now don't
tell us beggars that you will act for us, and then toss
us, as Mr. Mimerel proposes, 600,000 francs to keep us
quiet, like throwing us a bone to gnaw. We have other
claims. And anyway, we wish to bargain for ourselves
as other classes have bargained for themselves!"

And what can you say to answer that argument!

Perverted Law Causes Conflict

As long as it is admitted that the law may be diverted from its true purpose—that it may violate property
instead of protecting it—then everyone will want to
participate in making the law, either to protect himself
against plunder or to use it for plunder. Political questions will always be prejudicial, dominant, and all-ab-
sorbing. There will be fighting at the door of the Legislative Palace, and the struggle within will be no less
furious. To know this, it is hardly necessary to examine
what transpires in the French and English legislatures;
merely to understand the issue is to know the answer.

Bastiat based his analysis on the issue of ethics: a refusal to
use the state for the purpose of plunder.

This question of legal plunder must be settled once and for all, and there are only three ways to settle it:

The few plunder the many.

Everybody plunders everybody.

Nobody plunders anybody.

To understand correctly Bastiat's essay on the thing not seen, we must understand its connection to his idea of the state acting as an agency of plunder. He grounded his analysis of the economics of the broken window in terms of his broader concern: to persuade people not to adopt the politics of plunder.

He took a stand against the modern welfare statist's re-writing of God's commandment, "Thou shalt not steal." They have revised it as follows: "Thou shalt not steal, except by majority vote."

C. Hazlitt's Partial Use of Bastiat

We now return to Hazlitt's book. Hazlitt, following the lead of Bastiat, began with a violation of private property: the broken window. This act was a violation of ownership, but Hazlitt did not focus on the rights of ownership. In other words, he did not begin with the fundamental economic issue: "Who is legally responsible for the allocation of property, and why?" But there was a fundamental difference in Hazlitt's approach. He did not ground his criticism of state intervention in terms of ethics. He limited his use of the analogy of the broken window to this: a refutation of state intervention as the basis of economic growth.

Both men began with a negative sanction: throwing a stone through a window. This was a violation of property rights, but they never mentioned property rights. Had they done so, this would have raised the issue of ownership.

Then they followed the money. They showed that the owner had to re-allocate his financial budget to replace the broken window. Already, he was a loser. That was because he was a victim of a violent invasion of his rights of ownership.

Bastiat in *The Law* extended his critiques of state interventionism that he presented in his essay on the thing not seen. His criticism of the state in the essay was not grounded in morality. He merely traced the economic causes to their effects: a forced redistribution of wealth. Hazlitt picked up on this theme, but he did not adopt Bastiat's ethics-based refutation of state intervention, which he presented in *The Law*.

This is a fundamental difference between my book and Hazlitt's. I return to Bastiat's ethics-based analysis in *The Law*.

I begin with ownership. Specifically, I begin with God's ownership of all things. Men's ownership is delegated ownership. It is inherently a form of stewardship. This is a multi-phased stewardship: up to God, outward toward other participants in the economy, downward to those under his legal and also economic authority, and inward toward himself. Any violation of this stewardship is theft. It is a violation of ethics. So, by grounding my concept of ownership on the concept of God's ownership, I necessarily must invoke the issue of ethics: "Thou shalt not steal."

3. The Five-Point Structure of My Chapters

Hazlitt used Bastiat's broken window analogy as the analytical basis of his chapters. He followed the money analytically. He and Bastiat followed it back to the money owned by the window owner before someone tossed a stone through his window.

Beyond this general reliance on Bastiat's analytical procedure, Hazlitt followed no structure in his chapters. He was a clear writer. He was unique in this regard. But the chapters are not self-consciously structured in terms of a series of themes. I call these cookie-cutters. I use them all the time. Without these, it is difficult to recall the specifics of Hazlitt's arguments in each chapter.

I like to keep thing simple. So, I have adopted a five-point model. I cut each chapter into these five analytical cookies:

1. Owner
2. Window
3. Stone
4. Costs
5. Consequences.

I have written a book on this approach: *The Covenantal Structure of Christian Economics* (2015). I divide economics into these five categories:

1. Ownership
2. Stewardship
3. Law
4. Sanctions
5. Inheritance

In terms of social theory in general, these are as follows:

1. Sovereignty
2. Authority/hierarchy/representation
3. Ethics/law
4. Sanctions: positive and negative
5. Succession

The archetype is this:

1. God
2. Man
3. Law
4. Judgment
5. Time

I have written a book on this: *Unconditional Surrender* (5th ed., 2010).

I have worked with this structure since 1986. It affects much of my writing. It no doubt limits my thinking, but it also focuses my thinking. It makes it fairly easy to write rapid analyses, such as this book, which took a little under a hundred hours. I may miss lots of important issues, but these five are always the most important issues. Social theory that ignores any of these five points cannot be accurate. It is seriously incomplete.

By the way, just for the record, the Pentateuch is structured in terms of this framework:

Genesis (creation/sovereignty)
Exodus (hierarchy: Moses vs. Pharaoh)
Leviticus (laws)
Numbers (sanctions/war)
Deuteronomy (inheritance/conquest)

I wrote 16 of the 31 volumes of my economic commentary of the Bible to prove this, and then explore its implications.

For those of you who wonder where I got this structure, it was from a book published by my Institute for Christian Economics, Ray Sutton's *That You May Prosper* (1987). He derived it from Meredith Kline's *The Treaty of the Great King* (1963). Kline got it from George Mendenhall: *Law and Covenant in Israel and the Ancient Near East* (1955). I like to think that Mendenhall got it from God.

After you have read half a dozen of my chapters, you should be able to figure out in advance what I will say in each of the next chapters. As I say, I use a cookie cutter. Once you understand it, you will find that my analyses are straightforward.

Conclusion

Hazlitt did the grunt work in 1946. He, too, used a cookie cutter: Bastiat's analogy of the broken window. He had another at his disposal: Bastiat's concept of the politics of plunder. He did not pick it up and use it. I do.

I begin with point one: God is the original owner. My analysis there relates to the doctrine of subjective economic imputation: unitary, yet also corporate. God imputes value. I also cover economic stewardship (delegated ownership): individual, yet also corporate. I assume these doctrines in this book, but I do not expound them. I assume the existence of corporate judgment on corporate violations of private property.

Because God delegates ownership to individuals and institutions, this ownership is legitimate. It establishes ownership in society: a stewardship function. I begin here in each chapter: point one.

Point two is the window: the legal and institutional arrangements that are based on private ownership. Private ownership is a legal extension of the biblical concept of stewardship. God holds owners responsible for the administration of God's property. Thus, theft is an assault on God by way of His lawfully constituted legal and economic agents.

I identify the state's breaking of the window as an act of theft. It is a violation of God's legal boundaries around private property. I say what Hazlitt refused to say: state intervention into the private property order is organized theft. This is point three of my model: law.

Theft has consequences: sanctions. This is point four. I follow Hazlitt's lead in discussing the specific cause-and-effect outcomes of government intervention, chapter by chapter. This intervention makes most people poorer: the opposite of what promoters of government intervention promised the voters. Some people do get richer: the beneficiaries of the intervention.

The result of this reduction of wealth is reduced economic growth: point five of my model.

With this as background, you are ready for my book.

[Note: the 1979 edition of Hazlitt's book, published by Arlington House, included an extra chapter, listed as Chapter XVIII: "What Rent Control Does." It does not appear in the edition published in 2008 by the Mises Institute. It did not appear in the 1946 edition.]

Further Reading

For supporting material, go to bit.ly/CEIOL-Doc-Intro.

The Lesson

Thou shalt not steal (Exodus 20:15).

The Ten Commandments have ten points. The nice thing about each of them is this: it gets right to the point.

Christians disagree about which point this one is. Catholics and Lutherans believe that this is the seventh commandment. Most Protestants believe it is the eighth commandment. I am in this camp.

I am in the Eighth Commandment camp, but not because this is what most Protestants have always taught. I am in this camp for a very specific reason: I believe that the five points in the biblical covenant model are sequential. I believe that the third point has to do with boundaries, which include moral and legal boundaries. I wrote a four-volume commentary on the economics of the Book of Leviticus. Leviticus is the third book in the Pentateuch. I titled it, *Boundaries and Dominion.*

I realize this sequence was not understood prior to about 1954, with the publication of George Mendenhall's essay on Hittite suzerainty treaties. But once I understood this, after I read the manuscript of Ray Sutton's book, *That You May Prosper* (1987), I recognized the five-point structure with respect to the second set of five Commandments. The third commandment, "thou shalt not steal," has to do with boundary violations.

You do not have to accept my interpretation of the biblical covenant model in order for you to understand this book.

What I do want to consider is this: this commandment is short and sweet.

The Ten Commandments are aimed at all people. They are not aimed primarily at people with advanced degrees in the social sciences. The whole point of the Ten Commandments is this: *everyone is liable.* Nobody will be able to answer on judgment day with this response: "I just did not understand what this meant." Yes, he did. Not only did he understand it; he violated it.

It is significant that the first prohibition in the Bible is the prohibition on theft. God set up a tree in the midst of the garden, and He put a judicial boundary around it. Here was the declaration: "No trespassing." This was simple. This was not sophisticated. This was easily understood. And this is why, when temptation came, it was very specific. It was twofold. First, it promised knowledge that would elevate mankind in the understanding of good and evil. Second, it was a promise that nothing bad was going to happen if they stole the fruit.

So, they stole fruit.

It did not take a Ph.D. in economics to understand what was at stake here.

With this as background, I want to consider Chapter 1 of Hazlitt's book. I want to contrast it with what I am doing in this book.

1. Hazlitt's Definition of Economics

Hazlitt was a first-rate economist. He taught himself the basics of economics, and then he spent decades writing about economics. By 1946, he was prepared to write his book. I cannot think of anybody in the United States, or even the world, who could have written a better introductory book on economics in 1946.

Hazlitt offered a definition of good economics. He contrasted it with bad economics. He wanted to get these definitions clear in the minds of his readers.

> The bad economist sees only what immediately strikes the eye; the good economist also looks beyond. The bad economist sees only the direct consequences of a proposed course; the good economist looks also at the longer and indirect consequences. The bad economist sees only what the effect of a given policy has been or will be on one particular group; the good economist inquires also what the effect of the policy will be on all groups.

If we are talking about the logic of conventional economics, this is a good description of the two kinds of economics. I suspect that most economists would accept it. Each of them would, of course, assume that he is a representative of good economics. His critics, naturally, represent the bad economics faction. But the definition itself would probably be acceptable by most economists.

There is an enormous problem with this definition of good economics. It is this: *most people cannot follow long chains of reasoning.* Let me assure you, this includes most economists.

Hazlitt wrote the book to show that bad economics is based on inattention to a fairly simple concept. That concept is this: *the things not seen.* He used Bastiat's analogy of the broken window to drive home this point. His goal is simple to understand: *shorten the chains of reasoning.* He thought there are only two chains: the chain associated with the things seen, and the chain associated with the things not seen.

There is no question that his approach to explaining economics is excellent. This is why the book is still in print. This is why it still influences people who read it. They can better understand the second chain of reasoning: the things not seen.

Nevertheless, this does not overcome his definition's main problem: long chains of reasoning. Economists are highly sophisticated in denying the economic relevance of things not seen. They insist that their opponents have not seen the things which ought to be seen. They also insist that the things they have seen are the truly relevant things in understanding economics. Economists are masters at trying to persuade people—especially other economists—that what other economists see is not relevant.

The sophistication of these arguments can become remarkably complex. I am reminded of an old criticism of professional academics: "They use intellectual tools so sharp that the tools are useful only for splitting hairs."

Then there is this one: "Where there are five economists, there will be six opinions."

Hazlitt's approach always brings us back to this problem: the difficulty of following long chains of reasoning. I can think of no field in which this is a greater problem than it is in the field of economics. I do not mean economics among the masses. I mean economics among professional economists.

Hazlitt made a second point. He said that much of what is regarded as economic theory is in fact special pleading by special interest groups. Let us take this observation one step further. Special interest groups hire professional economists to do their special pleading. So, bad economists sign up. They are paid well to do this.

We are back to this problem: the average person is not in a position to assess which economist is the good economist. The average person is not in a position to follow the long chains of reasoning.

Hazlitt was accurate in saying the bad economists are the ones who ignore indirect consequences. But the trouble is, almost everybody who is trained in economics is skilled at guiding people down primrose paths. Long chains of reasoning are really more like primrose paths.

How is the average person expected to figure out which economist is a good economist, and which economist is a bad economist? How is he supposed to evaluate the special pleading of one group versus the special pleading of another group? This calls for a level of sophistication that the average man does not have.

This is the fundamental problem with Hazlitt's book. It is not that he was not a cogent economist. It is not that he was not a superb writer. It is simply this: readers are far less sophisticated than Hazlitt, let alone a small army of Ph.D.'s who promote Keynesianism.

Voters have to make decisions as to which special interest group is the right one to listen to. But voters really are not equipped to do this well. They get confused by long chains of reasoning.

They respond to slogans. The trick of the special interest group is to come up with a vote-getting slogan. Then it hires someone with a Ph.D. in economics to justify it.

We need better slogans. We can't beat something with nothing.

We also can't beat an eye-catching slogan with a long chain of reasoning.

I suggest this bumper sticker: **Thou shalt not steal**. This goes on the left-hand side of the bumper. This one goes on the right-hand side: **Even by majority vote**.

This leads me to my main point.

2. I Start With Ownership

This is why I do not start this book with Hazlitt's definition of a good economist. I start the book with this definition: the good economist understands the implications of ownership, and therefore he can identify theft.

The average voter is in a position to understand what theft is. He may not be able to follow long chains of reasoning, but he can understand this short chain of reasoning: "Thou shalt not steal." This is really all he needs to understand when it comes to understanding economics. If he gets this right, it will protect him from all of the primrose paths and all of the long chains of reasoning—incorrect reasoning.

Some economist may come up with a sophisticated formula that justifies state interference in the economy. He may come up with a graph. He may come up with just about anything that a creative mind can come up with. Those of us who are reading his presentation should ask ourselves this question: "Who wins, and who loses?" We should then ask ourselves this question: "If there were not somebody with a badge and a gun, with the gun pointing at one of the participant's belly, who would win, and who would lose?"

This book is about theft. It is also a book about badges and guns. This is the question of civil government.

The central economic question that every citizen should ask regarding civil government is this one: "Is the official who wears a badge and a gun truly acting in the name of the entire society, or is he acting on behalf of a special interest group?" If this book helps you answer this question accurately, then it is a successful book.

This is a book about badges and guns. This is also a book about ethics. This is a book about limiting the authority of people with badges and guns. This is the issue of state coercion. This book deals with the issue of state coercion and a social order based on the possibility of increased productivity. Above all, this is the issue of injustice.

We are back to the two issues raised by Bastiat.

"How God could have willed that men should attain prosperity only through Injustice and War? How He could have willed that they should be unable to avoid Injustice and War except by renouncing the possibility of attaining prosperity?"

God did not will this. Justice produces prosperity. Bastiat made this case. So does Deuteronomy 28:1-14.

Further Reading

For supporting material, go to bit.ly/CEIOL-Doc-1.

–2–

The Broken Window

Then Isaac sowed in that land, and received in the same year an hundredfold: and the LORD blessed him. And the man waxed great, and went forward, and grew until he became very great: For he had possession of flocks, and possession of herds, and great store of servants: and the Philistines envied him. For all the wells which his father's servants had digged in the days of Abraham his father, the Philistines had stopped them, and filled them with earth (Genesis 26:12–15).

I begin with a little-known passage in the Bible. The enemies of Abraham and his family resented the fact that Abraham had dug wells. Water wells are a major form of wealth in a low-rain society. Abraham had wealth; his son Isaac had wealth.

The Philistines resented this. So, when they had an opportunity to do so, they filled in the wells with dirt. This did not make them any wealthier. They did not steal the wells from Isaac. They also did not rent the wells from Isaac. They did not take advantage of the water. They simply made certain that Isaac could not take advantage of the water. This is the motivation we call envy. The translators of the Kings James Version recognized this. Envy is the motivation to destroy, to tear down. It targets an individual who has an advantage. The envious person does not seek to share in the advantage. He wants only to eliminate the other person's advantage.

Most of us find it difficult to believe that people are motivated in this way, but some people are, and they have been throughout history. They are filled with resentment.

This brings me to the topic at hand: the supreme lesson of Henry Hazlitt's book. When Hazlitt chose the title, *Economics in One Lesson*, he had to provide one lesson. The book has 24 chapters. But the title is an indication of what the book is about. Hazlitt only allowed himself one lesson.

Here is the lesson: Bastiat's broken window fallacy. Hazlitt chose that as his guide, which was an act of near genius. He discovered an idea that had been buried for a century. Bastiat's analogy was rather like Isaac's wells: filled in with dirt by Philistines. Hazlitt dug deep and got the water flowing again. Then he applied that principle in every chapter in the book. So, the title of the book is correct: he really does teach economics in one lesson. But it took 24 chapters to get this lesson across.

I take the broken window fallacy very seriously. Specifically, it is about envy. It is not about jealousy. This is why it is limited in dealing with those aspects of modern politics which we think of as the welfare state or wealth redistribution. Here is why. Envy is defined as the impulse of an individual who seeks to destroy somebody else's advantage, even though he is not benefited directly by the other person's loss.

Jealousy is different from envy. Jealousy is based on the recognition that somebody else has an advantage, but if you can apply some degree of coercion, maybe you can force the other person to share some of his advantage with you. This is the impulse of wealth redistribution by legislation. But envy is far more perverse. You cannot buy off the envious person by offering him something. You cannot make a deal with him. The very fact that you can offer him a benefit enrages him. It reminds him that you have what he does not have. He knows he is never going to have it, but he is determined to make certain that you do not have it either.

When societies adopt policies of wealth redistribution by the state, which do not increase wealth, but which make things more difficult for people who are wealthy, these policies are based on envy, not jealousy.

Bastiat's analogy begins with somebody who throws a stone through another person's window. This is an act of envy, not jealousy. Bastiat and Hazlitt did not spell this out, but we need to understand it from the beginning. It takes a self-conscious act of destruction to break a window. The window is not broken by a hurricane or other natural disaster. It is broken by somebody who resents the fact that somebody else owns a building with a window. In other words, this person has a deep-seated resentment against the owner.

Bastiat's goal for the analogy was simple: to help people understand that the money spent to repair a broken window has to come from somewhere. The cost of repairing the window is whatever the individual with the broken window must give up in order to repair the window. Whatever he spends to repair the window comes at the expense of whatever he would otherwise have done with the money.

This seems like a simple principle. But Hazlitt shows in 24 chapters that most voters do not perceive this fact: *state intervention of all kinds inaugurates the broken window process.* In other words, there are no free windows. This illustrates the fundamental principle of scarcity: there are no free lunches. Put differently, we cannot get something for nothing. This is a very important principle to understand. If it is true, then we had better look carefully at every political promise that a majority of voters can get something for nothing. Somewhere in the picture, there will be somebody's broken window.

I begin the discussion of the broken window with a discussion of who this somebody is. This somebody is the window's owner.

1. Owner

Ownership above all is *the right to exclude.* "This is mine. You can gain access to it only on my terms." Christian economics identifies when this right began. "And the Lord God commanded the man, saying, Of every tree of the garden thou mayest freely eat: But of the tree of the knowledge of good and evil, thou shalt not eat of it: for in the day that thou eat-est thereof thou shalt surely die" (Genesis 2:16–17). In short: "This tree is mine."

Someone owns the window. He may have purchased the building, and the building came with a window. Maybe he in-herited the building. Legally, he is the owner. He therefore is entitled to rights of ownership. These rights are defended by the society at large. They are honored by the society at large. They are defended by the civil government.

He has a right to this property. What does this mean? He has *legal immunity* from other people's theft or destruction of his property. He has *legal sovereignty*. The owner also has a legal right to defend his own property. Society grants him this right. More important for my discussion, *God grants him this right*. The owner is not alone (autonomous). He is not a lone wolf attempting to defend territory. *Ownership is a so-cial function.* Therefore, he has a moral right to the property, and this moral right is established by law: God's laws, society's customary law, civil law, and the individual's law.

I must make myself clear. The owner possesses *legal sover-eignty*. This is a matter of legal responsibility. Put differently, it is a matter of legal representation. He represents God. This legal sovereignty conveys *economic authority*. This means that he represents society economically. He is the recipient of con-stant bids for the use of his property. These bids come in the form of *prices*. There is no escape from this economic burden, other than selling the property.

The owner of the window enjoys the window. The window provides him with a stream of income. This income is psycho-logical. He enjoys light inside the building. The window lets in the light. The light is an economic asset. The window enables him to access this light during the day. It keeps the weather from getting inside the building. It also keeps out bugs and other critters. A window is a wonderful invention. We would hate to give up our windows, and this was especially true in 1850, before there was electrical light.

The owner has a legal immunity from violence. Nobody is allowed to steal his window. Nobody is allowed to throw a stone through his window. In other words, nobody is supposed to use violence against him by means of violence against the window.

The owner of the window makes several assumptions. He assumes that nobody is going to throw a stone through his window. He assumes that there be continuity in his life. The light will continue to shine in. The cold will continue to stay out. He trusts society in general to defend his interests. He makes decisions in terms of the assumption of continuity. This assumption of security rests on trust. If this trust is violated by an act of violence against him, although directed against his window, then his life will become less secure. He will not be able to make decisions in confidence. His future is more uncertain in a society in which the rights of ownership are not defended: by moral law, by custom, and by civil law.

2. Window

The window is not merely the capital asset. It is a representative asset. It points to ownership as such. It points to a social order that defends the rights of ownership. It points to a stable social order. Every piece of property is representative in this sense.

The owner is also a representative. He owns the building. He owns the window. He holds this in trust. He holds it in *legal* trust for God. He holds it in *economic* trust for society in general. The window represents a stable social order that is based on what we call property rights, but which are in fact rights of owners to enjoy whatever benefits a piece of property conveys to them.

The window has a price. This is why the person who throws the stone throws the stone. He wants to destroy the value of the property. The property has value, and this is reflected by its price. It has a price because there are other people who would like to own it. There are buyers out there who would like to buy the building and the window. The existence of a price testifies to demand for ownership. The competing bids of all those who would like to own the building and the window are what produce an objective price.

The free market has an economic rule: "high bid wins." This is the rule of every auction. The free market is a gigantic auction.

The highest bidder is the existing owner. He has to maintain this bid at all times. By not taking the highest bid among all the competing would-be owners, he forfeits the use of the money that the highest bidder would have given to him in exchange for the building and the window. So, as an owner, he must allocate the use of the building and the window. There is no escape from this economic responsibility.

The owner allocates a scarce resource. He allocates it to himself, but he does not do this at zero cost. He must forfeit whatever would have been offered in exchange for the building and the window. This decision costs him money. It costs him whatever the money would buy. This reminds him, day after day, that he must forfeit something for the ownership he enjoys.

I hope this is clear. This aspect of the free market is central to the social order. Somebody has to be held responsible for the administration of property. I argue that the owner is responsible to God. He is surely responsible to others in society. The social order that we know as free market capitalism legally links ownership and responsibility. It also links it economically. This is fundamental to the ability of the free market social order to produce both peace and wealth: *ownership and responsibility are linked.*

The two factors are linked economically by the free market because the person who owns the property must constantly pay to retain it. He pays specifically by forfeiting whatever would have been given to him in exchange for the property by the highest bidder in the marketplace. The owner may choose not to acknowledge this, but he bears this burden anyway. He must pay for his ownership. This is a social function. This is an economic function.

By linking ownership and responsibility, the free market forces owners to take responsibility. They must pay to retain their ownership. Other people in the society have a legal right to make bids for ownership. They are owners of whatever they own. They can offer to exchange it.

In making a higher bid than previously manifested in the marketplace, the new bidder increases the degree of responsibility in the life of the owner. The owner must now pay even more than he did before to retain ownership. This is an efficient way for any society to make sure that every piece of private property is administered in terms of the highest bids in the society. A man retains ownership of whatever he owns, but never at zero price.

The window is a physical manifestation of this responsibility. This is why it is a great analogy. It lets in the light. The light makes it easier for us to see what is going on around us.

3. Stone

Along comes an envy-driven person. He resents the fact that someone owns the building and the window. He is determined to get even with that person. He cannot get even by buying the building. He does not have the money to buy the building. But he can still get even. He can break the window. He can undermine the value of the building by destroying the window. This suits him just fine.

So, he picks up a stone, which is readily available. In the dark of night, he throws the stone through the window, and then he runs. No one sees him do it. He does not get caught, although he risks getting caught.

The man who owns the building now faces a problem. Much of the value of the building is dependent upon a functioning window. He is now going to have to replace the window. He wants the light to stream back in, but now he must pay for it.

How is he going to pay for it? He is going to have to get

access to money, which he may have in a savings account. Or he may have to sell something else that he owns in order to get money. But he is going to have to get money because he has to pay somebody to replace the window. There are no free windows.

Someone has violated his right of ownership. This also must be paid for. He now knows he is vulnerable. Somebody in the community resents him. Somebody in the community is willing to violate his rights of ownership. It is not just that the broken window is going to let the cold come in, or the flies and mosquitoes come in. He has lost more than this. He has lost the security that he thought he enjoyed because someone in the community is driven by envy. Someone in the community figured out that he could impose a loss on the owner at zero cost to himself. He threw the stone, and he escaped into the darkness.

The owner had enjoyed the continuity of light streaming in, and no bugs streaming in. He enjoyed the continuity of security. He had thought that his ownership was secure, and now it is not.

The person who threw the stone did not just break a window. He broke trust that was associated with the window. If this continues, or if it is imitated, this can disrupt society. This is not mere academic speculation. One of the major breakthroughs in law enforcement in the 20th century was the recognition of the existence of a broken window phenomenon in the community. If a building is abandoned, and vandals begin throwing rocks through the windows, the crime rate goes up. One of the best indicators of a declining part of town is the existence of broken windows in abandoned buildings. This breakdown in social order can become a downward spiral: more broken windows leading to greater crime.

To reverse this, it takes more than a police force. There has to be individual commitment within the neighborhood to put a stop to it. The broken windows reflect a decline in community commitment. When a community will not defend private property, the community is going to experience greater crime and economic setbacks. This is most clearly manifested in broken windows. Bastiat's analogy is not just an analogy. It is a representative case.

4. Costs

The owner must pay to replace the window. This sets off a chain of economic events.

The general public recognizes that the owner must spend money to repair the window. Some people, who may regard themselves as budding economists, will argue that this spending increases employment locally. The person who repairs the window has to buy the glass. He has to pay employees. So, this is good for the community, the budding economists conclude.

The analogy of the broken window informs us that this is not good for the community. It is good for the repairman and those employed by him, but it is not good for the community. There are costs associated with the repairs.

The owner has to pay for the repairs. Any money that he was going to spend on something else must now be spent on replacing the broken window. We do not get something for nothing. There are no free lunches, and there are no free windows. The cost to the owner of the broken window is the cost of *the most valued use he had for the money,* which he must now pay to the window repairman.

By making this insight clear, Bastiat performed a wonderful service for people in search of economic understanding. But he did not go far enough. The cost extends beyond the window owner. There is a cost for the community. There has been a disruption in one owner's life. He had hoped for a safe enjoyment of light coming through the window, and cold and mosquitoes not coming through the window. That confidence has now been broken. There is now an element of society that does not honor the rights of ownership. Everybody is put at risk. There is a decline in trust. People do not trust each other as much as they did before. They may decide to hire somebody else on the payroll of the police department. Everybody's costs of operation go up.

The person who threw the stone targeted a window, but his real target was the owner of the window. We should also recognize that he had more than this target. He was targeting anybody in the community who owns a window. This is a classic example of the phrase, "two birds with one stone." There were far more than two birds. There were more victims than the owner of the broken wibdow. He was targeting the social order. He was targeting the confidence that people have in their rights as property owners. That stone did not just break the window; it broke people's trust in the stability of the social order. If the stone thrower is imitated, trust will be reduced even more.

The analogy of the broken window is excellent in pointing out that there are costs to the owner. But if we pursue this analogy, we will see that there are costs far beyond those born by the owner of the window.

5. Consequences

The stone thrower sent a message to the community. The community now knows that the rights of property are now at risk. A new attitude is now loose in the community. It is an attitude that is hostile to economic inequality. It is hostile to individual wealth. It is hostile to the idea that somebody should enjoy the fruits of his labor, including the fruits of his knowledge. Everybody's property is now at risk, which is another way of saying that everybody's legal rights are at risk.

At this point, people have to make decisions. Is this a trend? Will there be more stones thrown through other windows? Is it time to start allocating money to a larger police force? Is it time to start spending money on private security services? Is it time to buy lights that go on automatically when somebody is in the yard? Is it time to buy security cameras?

It is now more expensive to defend the rights of ownership. It is not just that one person has suffered a loss associated with replacing a broken window. It is that the entire community is now going to have to consider a new threat to individual wealth. People are going to have to think about their budgets. If they want to avoid the cost of replacing a broken window, they may have to expend more money in crime prevention in the community. The costs of living in that community will go up. Money which would have been allocated for consumer spending or for investing will now have to be spent on the protection of property.

What we saw in the case of the individual who was the victim of the stone, namely, that he must now spend money to repair the window, is repeated throughout the community. People who would rather have spent the money on something else now decide that it is time to spend the money on self-defense. This increases the cost of living. This reduces people's wealth. More important, it reduces their sense of security. Uncertainty rises. Dealing with uncertainty costs money. That is to say, people must forfeit the use of whatever they would have rather done with their money because they now have to spend money to defend their property.

This reduces the value of property. If owners must spend more money to defend it, the net return from owning it falls. This reduces the value and the price of property.

This decline will reduce thrift. If the present value of consumer goods declines, then their future value will be lower if people think attacks on property will continue. People will not save money to invest today if the value of future property is expected to be lower.

If you thought a stone thrower might visit your house, would you save up for double-pane windows, or would you buy a chain-link fence and a large guard dog?

Conclusion

The logic of the broken window does not simply apply to the broken window. It also does not simply apply to the owner of the now-broken window. It applies to the whole community.

Let me give another example. Somebody tosses a stone into a quiet lake. He can watch the ripples spread from the stone across the lake. The tranquility of the lake is disrupted. The predictability of the lake is reduced. This does not hurt anybody's ownership. This is not a threat to the community. It is even aesthetically appealing. It is not directed against a piece of capital equipment that produces predictable benefits for the owner. It is not a threat to the community at large. But there are ripple effects.

There are also ripple effects when somebody throws a stone through a window. The tranquility of the community has been disrupted. The predictability of ownership has been reduced. We must look not simply at the cost borne by the owner of the original window. We must also look at the cost borne by other individuals—society in general. Other individuals have been the victims of the stone thrower.

The remaining chapters in this book will consider the comprehensive costs of violence against property owners.

Further Reading

For supporting material, go to bit.ly/CEIOL-Doc-2.

The Blessings of Destruction

If fire break out, and catch in thorns, so that the stacks of corn, or the standing corn, or the field, be consumed therewith; he that kindled the fire shall surely make restitution (Exodus 22:6).

This passage has to do with legal liability. If somebody sets a fire on his own property, and this fire spreads to his neighbor's property, the man who set the fire is legally responsible. He has to make restitution to his victim. This is a case of accidental damage. How much greater is the liability when the damage is deliberate?

The Bible makes it clear that ownership involves legal responsibility. An owner is responsible for his property-based actions. He is not entitled to pass on his costs of ownership to his neighbor, unless his neighbor has given permission. His neighbor has been granted legal immunity for his property. This is a legal boundary. No one is allowed to invade his property. This is not just geographical property; this is any form of property.

Here, we see that the Bible teaches a concept of profit and loss. The owner of the initial field hopes to benefit in some way from lighting a fire on his property. This is a cost of operation. This is a risk. He is not allowed to transfer this risk to his neighbor. It is clear that in the case of a fire, his neighbor has suffered damages. The man who started the fire is legally responsible for the damages inflicted on the neighbor. This is a concept of strict liability.

There is not a hint in this text that neighborhoods are benefit-ed by fires that get out of control. There is not a sense of the idea that invading another person's property can take place at zero cost to either society or the victim. If this is true of an accidental fire, how much greater is the liability in the case of an arsonist?

With this as background, let us study the example of a per-verse idea: the idea that inflicting destruction creates wealth. Hazlitt began with the issue of war. In 1946, this was in every-body's mind. The world had just come through a devastating conflagration in which something in the range of 60 million people had died. He began with popular opinion, including the great captains of industry, chambers of commerce, labor union leaders, and editorial writers.

> Though some of them would disdain to say that there are net benefits in small acts of destruction, they see almost endless benefits in enormous acts of destruc-tion. They tell us how much better off economically we all are in war than in peace. They see "miracles of pro-duction" which it requires a war to achieve. And they see a postwar world made certainly prosperous by an enormous "accumulated" or "backed-up" demand.

He then reminded the reader: "It is merely our old friend, the broken-window fallacy, in new clothing, and grown fat be-yond recognition."

The assumption underlying the fallacy is that backed-up demand is a positive force in society. This demand has come about as a result of the prior destruction. Hazlitt went on to explain that just because people would like to own something that had been destroyed does not produce demand. Only their productivity produces demand. As in the case of the man with the broken window, this productivity will be used to purchase goods and services that the owner of the recently destroyed goods would not otherwise have purchased, had his goods not been destroyed.

1. Owner

The owner of the broken goods was a victim of violence. The war had invaded his property. He is now poorer than he had been before the war began. He had owned property that was in good working order. He now owns a pile of rubble. He has suffered a major loss.

Had his next-door neighbor started a fire on his own property, and the fire had spread to his neighbor's property, the fire-starter would owe restitution. The victim would be compensated for his loss. Because he had been made poorer by the fire, he is legally entitled to restitution from the person who started the fire. There is no sense in which the owner of the burned-over property is better off than he was before the fire. Similarly, there is no sense in which the owner of rubble is better off because the war invaded his property.

An owner has responsibilities in life. These responsibilities led him to accumulate property before the war. Now this property is destroyed. This reduction of personal responsibility has taken place through no fault of his own. But, to the extent that his property had enabled him better to fulfill his responsibilities, whether to God, his family, his community, or himself, he is now less able to fulfill those responsibilities than he had been prior to the war.

As an owner, he had been the beneficiary of multiple streams of income from his capital goods. He no longer has these streams of income because he no longer has functioning capital goods. He is poorer in terms of income than he had been before the war. He is less able to fulfill his responsibilities in life.

He also has a new concern. Will there be another war? Will his property be invaded again? Should he accumulate property that is easily destroyed in wartime? Should he allocate his property, such as labor, into forms of capital which, if he were confident of continuing peace, he would not consider? His life has been disrupted by the war, and not simply in the past. The war has reminded him of his own vulnerability. He must now consider allocations of his capital that will reduce his consumption or reduce his productivity, but which are necessary to protect him against another outbreak of violence.

2. Window

As an owner of capital, he had served the community. Scarce economic resources have economic value. We know this because they command prices in the market. Somebody is willing to bid for either ownership or the use of the resources. Somebody must make the decision regarding who should have access to these resources. Who should have access to the income streams or the streams of production that are generated by this property? Such decisions are not made at zero cost. Somebody has to be economically responsible for them. Somebody has to make decisions in terms of the highest bids of consumers or their economic agents, entrepreneurs.

Before the war, the owner had decided that he would make the highest bids to retain ownership. He therefore forfeited the use of whatever money or wealth that the highest bidder for everything he owned would have paid him. That was his cost of operation. In terms of his own hierarchy of values, both moral and economic, he allocated wealth to retain ownership of his property.

If this property provided income for him, then he was able to make voluntary exchanges with other people. But now his tools of production are broken. Now he cannot afford to make these exchanges. The productivity that his tools of production had previously provided him is missing in action.

To say that he is better off now than he was before the war is ludicrous. Hazlitt's argument shows that he is not better off. Now he must spend money or time to replenish his stock of capital. He may make these expenditures, but the cost of these expenditures ought to be clear: whatever he would otherwise have purchased, had the war not invaded his property. The broken tools of production, analytically speaking, are exactly like the broken window. He is the victim of violence.

There is no pent-up demand. There may be post-war demand, because the victim needs to replace his broken property. But this demand would have been manifested even if there had been no war. It simply would have been manifested in other areas of the economy. Total demand is less than it would otherwise have been, because the wealth of the person going into markets and attempting to buy goods and services is less than it was prior to the war.

3. Stone

The implements that were used to destroy his property were weapons. They were deliberately designed to break things. He has been the victim of concentrated violence. He has been the victim of violence imposed on a systematic basis. In this case, the destroyer's motivation was not envy. His motivation was destruction for the sake of the official causes of the war.

There is no doubt that war is destructive. It is certainly more destructive than a stone thrown at midnight by an envy-driven vandal. The war's victim has suffered greater loss than the stone would have inflicted on him.

It may be that he was not the direct victim. But he was forced to pay taxes to support the war effort. He is therefore poorer than he would have been if he had not had to pay those taxes. There is no pent-up demand.

4. Costs

The costs of replacing the rubble with new capital equipment must be borne by somebody. There are no free lunches. There is no free capital. Somebody must pay.

The net wealth of the victims of the war is lower than it was before the war. So, demand registered by the victims in those markets associated with the removal of rubble and the building of new structures may be higher than it was prior to the war. But this means that demand registered by the victims in those many markets that are not associated with removing the rubble and building new structures will be reduced.

Meanwhile, the victims will live in terrible conditions. They will suffer greatly. They are no doubt highly motivated to remove the rubble and rebuild living quarters. But unless they find resources in terms of their own labor, meaning opportunities to serve the general community within the framework of a free market, they will not be able to register this demand in a way that promotes economic growth.

There is no escape from the cost of destruction. Destruction imposes unexpected costs on victims. To imagine that these victims will be better off because they will live in new buildings is to imagine that they are now better off than they would have been, had their homes not been destroyed. But the very fact that they did not tear down the old buildings and replace them before the war began indicates that they are in a less desirable situation today, after the war, than they had been before the war. They are now forced to buy what they did not want to buy. They have had to re-budget, not because they are better off, but because they are worse off.

5. Consequences

Before the war, there had been considerable productivity because of the existing capital base of society. After the war, this capital base is smaller than it was before the war. So, the productivity of the population is less after the war than before the war. The consequences for society should be obvious: *reduced wealth per capita.* Society has less capital than it did before, and therefore the only way that per capita income would be higher, would be as a result of deaths inflicted during the war. To argue that the society is better off under such conditions, since it has higher per capita wealth, would be recognized as ludicrous. Members of families that had lost loved ones in the war do not regard themselves as better off than they were before the war, simply because in particular instances, a family's per capita capital is higher.

A family that lived in a rural area in Germany during World War II may not have suffered greatly. No bombs fell on it.

No troops invaded. The family may have had a small farm, and therefore had access to meat, butter, and other consumer goods that were regarded as delicacies by the end of the war. But if that family lost a husband or a son during the war, as a result of conscription, the widows did not regard themselves as better off because of a higher ratio of per capita investment.

The division of labor shrinks during a bombing raid. Specialization shrinks as a result of the reduced division of labor. The capital that it will require to recover from war will have to be allocated as a result of much greater thrift. Prior to the war, this degree of thrift was not mandatory, for the society had an inherited legacy: capital that had been built up for decades or even longer. After the war, that capital is gone. So, whatever capital is replenished through much greater thrift could have been invested before the war, meaning that it could have been added to a far larger capital base.

A society that has experienced bombing raids, invasions by millions of troops, and losses of life as a result of battlefield deaths and civilian disease is not richer than it was before the war.

Hazlitt understood this in 1946. Those American businessmen who imagined that there would be pent-up European economic demand because of the war, which in turn would benefit them, did not count the costs of the war. They did not count the costs to individuals. They also did not count the costs to the social order due to a shrinking division of labor.

Conclusion

A variant of this argument applies to natural disasters. After a tornado or earthquake levels a community, there will be an article about the stimulative economic effects of the disaster. Former homeowners will have to rebuild. This, we are assured, is positive economically. The victims will own newer buildings. The local economy will boom.

The inability of people to recognize the existence of the things unseen is at the heart of their economic ignorance. Hazlitt was wise to resurrect Bastiat's analogy of the broken window. He made the correct point with respect to pent-up demand. "But need is not demand. Effective economic demand requires not merely need but corresponding purchasing power."

If Christians took seriously the biblical law of fire-starting, they would be less likely to make such a conceptual error. The Bible does not mandate economic restitution for acts that increase the wealth of third parties. It mandates restitution for acts that decrease the wealth of third parties.

War decreases the wealth of third parties.

Further Reading

For supporting material, go to bit.ly/CEIOL-Doc-3.

–4–

Public Works Mean Taxes

For the lips of a strange woman drop as an honeycomb, and her mouth is smoother than oil: But her end is bitter as wormwood, sharp as a two-edged sword (Proverbs 5:3–4).

The author of Proverbs in the first nine chapters contrasts the faithful wife with the strange woman. He uses the metaphor of the strange woman for alluring lies that ultimately betray the person who accepts them. Here is the passage's underlying message: something can look very appealing on the surface, but the end thereof is bitter as wormwood. Why? Because there is a system of moral cause and effect in history. When someone violates fundamental ethical principles, he will eventually experience negative sanctions. This is also true of entire social orders.

This passage has economic implications. The specific ethical context of the passage is this commandment: "Thou shalt not commit adultery." But the general ethical context of the passage also applies to this commandment: "Thou shalt not steal." This in turn applies to government spending. The passage in Proverbs warns us against all versions of the economic error that Bastiat called "the thing not seen"—the true economic cost of our actions.

This chapter deals with public works projects. These are projects that are funded by the state. They are highly visible. They look very productive. It is relatively easy to gain public support for the construction of these projects. On the surface, they look appealing, but the end thereof is bitter as worm-wood: higher taxes. But the wormwood goes far deeper than higher taxes, as we shall see. There are several layers of things not seen.

The appeal of public works is the appeal of something for nothing. It is the appeal of the devil's temptation of Jesus: stones into bread (Matthew 4:3). The voters are told that a public works project will do two things. First, it will create employment. Second, it will create wealth. Whenever we hear such an appeal, we should remember the principle: "There are no free lunches." This is the underlying reality of the things not seen—plural.

With this in mind, let us return to the familiar five-point model of the fallacy of the broken window.

1. Owner

I begin with the biblical principle of private ownership. This principle is manifested twice in the Ten Commandments: the prohibition on objective theft and the prohibition on sub-jective coveting. We are to respect the judicial boundaries of ownership. This has to do with ethics: moral and legal bound-aries.

Throughout this book, I am trying to make clear that there are two issues here: judicial sovereignty and economic author-ity. These are separate concepts. They are also inescapably re-lated concepts. Judicial sovereignty is primary.

The fundamental principle of ownership in the biblical con-text is this: there is a tight judicial connection between own-ership and personal responsibility. This is a matter of *judicial sovereignty*: the legal rights of ownership. These legal rights establish immunity. They establish legal boundaries.

Economic theory informs us that there is also a tight eco-nomic connection between ownership and personal respon-sibility. This has to do with economic costs. When an asset owner uses it for one purpose, he cannot use it for another. The highest-value forfeited use is his cost of ownership. This cost cannot be avoided. This is a matter of *economic authority*. It is an inescapable implication of judicial sovereignty: the legal right to use the resources we own, which therefore is the *legal right to exclude others*. There are inevitable personal costs associated with ownership; there are also personal benefits. Jesus said that we must count the costs (Luke 14:28-30).

An individual owns an asset. Civil law upholds this claim. He is convinced that he is responsible before God and other people for the use of this asset. It is part of his wealth. He may see that he is responsible for the increase of his wealth. Maybe he has read the 25th chapter of the Gospel of Matthew, which presents the parable of the talents.

Ownership is always tied economically to allocation. It has to do with budgeting. Any scarce economic resource that is used for one thing cannot be used for another thing. The owner must choose. There is no escape from this judicial responsibility. There is also no escape from this economic responsibility.

Under biblical law, and also under free market institutions, an owner has a sense of ownership. He believes that he owns the legal right to use an asset. *Ownership is a bundle of legal rights.* By rights, I mean *legal immunities from coercion*. This means legal immunities from private coercion, and it also means legal immunities from state coercion.

This assumption of ownership rights permeates every aspect of the free market economy. It permeates every aspect of individual economic decision-making. This is the foundation of the free market social order. This legal foundation is taught in the Bible, and Christian economic analysis must take this into consideration.

We know the phrase posted in retail shops: "If you break it, you own it." This means that if you break it, you must pay for it. But there is another side of ownership: "If you own it, you may legally break it." Both must be affirmed: purchase and use. When you buy it, you also buy the bundle of rights that legally comes with it.

2. Window

The window in this case is each individual's net wealth. Individuals believe that they lawfully possess wealth. This wealth is not simply the money that an owner could generate by selling all of his assets. This wealth is also very much a matter of his *legal immunity from coercion.* It is the wealth associated with property rights.

The Bible teaches that men are legal agents of God. It also teaches that one of the ways that this legal responsibility is manifested is through ownership. This makes owners stewards of God. This is hierarchical. But this economic stewardship also has what we call horizontal aspects. Owners are stewards for third parties. Third parties bid for ownership. The result of these bids is an array of prices. Would-be owners shout to owners: "Sell it to me!" or "Let me rent it!" *Wherever there is a price, there we find economic stewardship.* This is inescapable. The owner is an economic agent of society. He decides who gets to use whatever he owns, and also on what terms. This is an inescapable economic implication of judicial sovereignty.

People make decisions in terms of what they perceive to be immunity from taxation. They believe that they have the legal obligations and also the economic opportunities associated with ownership. To increase their wealth, they must participate in the social division of labor. This leads them to cooperate with others. They make decisions in terms of whatever they want to buy. Whatever they want to buy is closely related to whatever they have to offer in exchange. There are no free lunches.

The exchange system in a free market economy extends the division of labor. People make decisions regarding the allocation of their wealth, and they do so in terms of their perceptions of opportunities for service: their opportunities to serve others, but also others' opportunities to serve them. This focus on service comes from an inevitable aspect of stewardship in a world of scarce resources: asset allocation.

To achieve their goals at a low cost, they have to gain cooperation from other people, especially strangers. The main way that they do this is to offer opportunities to these people. We are back to Adam Smith's famous dictum: we should not expect to gain what we want from the butcher or the baker based on an appeal to their charitable instincts. We should expect to gain cooperation on the basis of this offer: "I will provide what you want, if you will provide me with what I want."

In other words, the value of the window is not simply the benefits that the window will provide in terms of letting light in and keeping cold and bugs out. It is also the right of ownership that someone has with respect to his window. Specifically, it is *his* window. It is not somebody else's window. This fact of ownership, he believes, entitles him to the use of his window. This legal right of use, which inescapably means *the right to exclude others*, may be of much greater value to him than the benefits expected from the window itself.

Wealth gives owners greater freedom of action. Wealth, when combined with legal immunities from coercion, leads asset owners to make specific allocation decisions. They count the costs and benefits of their decisions. They seek cooperation. They want to participate in the social division of labor. All of this is threatened by a deliberately tossed stone.

3. Stone

The analogy of the stone represents an illegal invasion of a boundary. The boundary is a property right. One more time: by property right, I mean the legal immunity from coercion with respect to personal wealth.

In the case of public works, the stone has the characteristic features of the strange woman. It has great allure. This is not simply a stone picked up at random, and then tossed through a window out of spite or out of envy. This particular stone is based on a conceptual model. It may be based on a physical working model, but the conceptual model is the key. It is a model of great beauty. It is something to be desired. It offers specific benefits to the person who takes advantage of it. The benefits are obvious; the costs are deliberately concealed.

There are always hidden costs of this stone. Always, the benefits must be paid for. Specifically, the benefits must be paid for by specific people. Somebody is going to benefit from a particular public works project. But somebody else is going to have to pay for it. In some cases, this may be the same person, but in all likelihood, the person making the decision to toss the stone sees that he will gain more from the outcome of the stone tossing then he will pay.

This is not a matter of envy: the destruction of what someone else owns. Rather, this is a matter of jealousy: the desire to get part of what someone else owns. The underlying assumption of the stone-thrower is this: "Somebody else is going to have to pay more to get the benefits than I will have to pay." There is no question regarding the underlying economics of this relationship: it is theft.

4. Costs

The most important cost of state intervention into the economy, rarely discussed, is this one: *the state's violation of property rights.* The taxpayer has been subjected to a loss. His immunity from coercion has been reduced. His wealth is more uncertain than it was before. The arbitrariness of the state now threatens the future predictability of his personal plans.

With a public works project, the state has tossed the stone through the windows of taxpayers. The state has therefore forced existing taxpayers to adopt new budgets. These budgets are not what each of these taxpayers would have chosen, had the state not started some public works project, and had the state not been forced to tax certain individuals in the general public. Each taxpayer would have made individual allocation decisions in terms of his original budget. Now he must re-think his decisions in terms of a different, smaller budget. Taxpayers would have made their plans in terms of personal balance sheets; now they are forced by state coercion to make their decisions in terms of reduced balance sheets. The ability of individuals to achieve their personal goals is reduced when the tax bills come due.

Politicians promote a pubic works project in terms of benefits that will be seen. The exact details of who is going to pay for these benefits are always kept in the background. Politicians do not want voters to make a careful analysis of the real costs of the project. They persuade the voters that the costs will be born by somebody else, or at least most of the costs will be born by somebody else.

Another major loss is the reduction of voluntary cooperation. People would have made different plans, and they would have coordinated these plans with different people. The new public works project will no doubt foster new kinds of exchange relationships. Some people will be benefitted. But the question is this: Will a social order based on voluntary cooperation be extended by state compulsion into the economy? Unfortunately, hardly anybody ever asks this question.

There will be new employment in those areas associated with the public works project. But there will also be reductions in employment in all of those areas where the taxpayers' money would otherwise have been spent, but which now is spent by the state. We see the benefits; we do not see the losses. We see people employed on the public works projects; we do not see the people who are not employed because there are no private works projects as a result of the taxes.

Another major aspect of this that is rarely discussed is this: What is it going to cost to keep the public work in repair? Maintenance costs are inevitable. Who is going to bear the burden of these costs? Even when a fee is attached to a public work, such as a toll bridge or a toll road, we find that there is political maneuvering by other groups to get their hands on the flow of income generated by the fees. This has been basic to modern politics for a century or more.

5. Consequences

The first and most important consequence is this: *the re-*

duced security of property. Put in terms of legal terms, it means a reduced area of responsibility for individuals. They now must allocate more resources than before to protecting their property. These resources could have been used for other purposes—purposes that were higher on taxpayers' individual lists of priorities. But because of the violation of their property rights, these priorities must now be placed lower on their lists. In other words, there is *diluted ownership*, and therefore there is *diluted responsibility*.

The biblical principle of personal ethics is this: *increased personal responsibility*. The message of the Bible is clear: there will be no plea-bargaining at the final judgment. This is the message of the parable of the talents. The concept of public works projects undermines personal responsibility. "Blame the committee!" There are no committees at the final judgment.

After the tax bills arrive, productive people will begin to allocate more resources to tax avoidance and away from economic production. Resources will go to lawyers and accountants rather than engineers and marketers. This is good news for lawyers and accountants, but bad news for the general public. Productivity will decline.

There will be a reduction in the division of labor. The division of labor is extended by voluntary cooperation. People learn to trust other individuals and companies over extended periods of time. They establish personal networks. People trust each other with respect to all kinds of projects. But this zone of personal interdependence is thwarted by increased taxation.

This is all the consequence of ignoring the reality of the things not seen. Voters are mesmerized by the vision of the benefits generated by the public works. They see benefits flowing for decades or longer. But they do not see the costs.

The popularity of the things seen is likely to lead to the construction of more public works. There will be more government stones tossed through more privately owned windows. Property rights will be violated again and again. The negative consequences of this are inevitable. Sometimes, we are wise enough to call them what they are: unintended consequences.

Sometimes they are called side effects. We forget what should be obvious: there are no side effects. There are only effects. The effects we do not like are the ones we call side effects.

One of these effects, which we like to call side effects, is this: *taxes discourage production.* I will cover this in the next chapter.

Conclusion

The strange woman in economics today is seen by most Christians as a biblically faithful social order. They have accepted as biblical the ancient error of government-funded public works projects as economically productive in the aggregate.

Public works projects are state subsidies to one group of citizens. These subsidies are paid for by taxpayers. The benefits are visible. The taxes are paid in private. There will be an organized constituency behind a public works project. There will be no such organized constituency behind the taxpayers.

Just as with a strange woman, a public works project starts wearing out as soon as it is introduced to respectable society. Many of the voters who once enjoyed its benefits will inevitably grow bored. There are always newer, more alluring projects. Eventually, it will need the equivalent of a facelift. But even a facelift does not help. It still sags. The wrinkles get worse. Hardly anyone comes to visit any more. Someday, it will have to be replaced. The key question is this: Will the replacement be another strange woman?

Men should have better taste. They should adopt a more long-run view. They should count all of the costs of their actions: the things not seen. But they don't. That is why there are authoritative commandments to remind them in times of great temptation. They all boil down to this: "Don't."

Further Reading

For support material, go to bit.ly/CEIOL-Doc-4.

5

Taxes Discourage Production

And he will take the tenth of your seed, and of your vineyards, and give to his officers, and to his servants. And he will take your menservants, and your maidservants, and your goodliest young men, and your asses, and put them to his work. He will take the tenth of your sheep: and ye shall be his servants. And ye shall cry out in that day because of your king which ye shall have chosen you; and the Lord will not hear you in that day. (I Samuel 8:15–18).

The people of Israel wanted a king. They heard of the nations around them, and they were told that these nations had strong central governments. Each was led by a king, who embodied the power, prestige, and glory of his nation-state. The system of civil rule in Israel at this time was based on decentralized tribes. Each tribe had a system of judges. There was no legislature. There was no central civil government.

Samuel was both a priest and a civil judge. Representatives of the people of Israel came to him and asked him to anoint someone to serve as a king. He warned them against this. His warning came in the form of a threat: increased taxation. Not only would they have to pay taxes to the local tribal civil governments, they would now have to pay taxes to the central government, as embodied by the king.

Nevertheless the people refused to obey the voice of Samuel; and they said, Nay; but we will have a king

49

over us; That we also may be like all the nations; and that our king may judge us, and go out before us, and fight our battles (vv. 19–20).

We might think that the threat of increased taxation would have scared them off. Not so. They wanted to be represented by someone with power, and they were willing to pay the price. The price was an additional tax of 10% of their income.

This 10% figure was the same as the tithe that was owed to the Levites, the tribe of the priesthood. Samuel warned them that the king would extract as much wealth from them as the entire priestly tribe was entitled to. This centralization of wealth and power would be enormous. But they did not care. They wanted a powerful central state, so they got one. It lasted through four kings. During the early years of the fourth king, Rehoboam, a tax revolt took place. The nation of Israel separated into the northern and southern kingdoms (I Kings 12). It was never brought together again under the rule of a Hebrew king.

The threatened system of taxation was proportional. It followed the same rule as the principle of the tithe. Everybody paid the same percentage. No group within the society would be able to extract a greater percentage of wealth from a richer group. The economic burden that afflicted the rich would also afflict the poor. The king of Israel would be an equal opportunity exploiter. Nevertheless, the people demanded a king.

It was clear that the productivity of the people of Israel would decline under the rule of the centralized government as manifested by a single king. A tenth of their wealth would be extracted every year. In addition, he would take menservants and maidservants away from them. These servants would no longer be part of the household production system. The wealth that they would otherwise have produced would be transferred to the king and his household. The households would no longer be as productive, because the resource inputs available to them would be siphoned off by the king. Nevertheless, the people demanded a king.

We take away two lessons from this. First, people who are in ethical rebellion prefer tyranny to liberty. This came as no surprise to Samuel, for God had told him that this would be the case.

> And the Lord said unto Samuel, Hearken unto the voice of the people in all that they say unto thee: for they have not rejected thee, but they have rejected me, that I should not reign over them (v. 7).

Second, they are not swayed by the argument that higher taxes will reduce their wealth. They prefer to live under the embodiment of power rather than enjoy greater personal productivity. They did not listen to the economic logic of Samuel. He was correct in his assessment, but they paid no attention.

This is always the problem with voters who criticize the existing tax code. They do not object to taxation as such. They are happy to extend power to the central government. They just want a different tax code, so that someone else will have to bear a greater burden of taxation. They reject the principle of the tithe: proportional taxation. They think they can use their influence so that the central government will extract greater wealth from those who have more income than they do. Their call for tax reform is this: "Don't tax you. Don't tax me. Tax the guy behind the tree."

1. Owner

Private ownership is based on a legal connection between ownership rights—legal immunities from theft—and personal responsibility. In the biblical worldview, God grants ownership to an individual. He thereby increases the individual's personal responsibility.

Ownership provides a test of performance: ethical and economic. The owner has a responsibility to increase his wealth on behalf of God, the original owner This was taught by Jesus in the parable of the talents (Matthew 25:14-30). The original owner delegates the responsibilities of asset management to three men. Later, he returns for an accounting. He sees if each of them has increased the owner's wealth. Two did; one did not. The two who did are then given greater wealth—redistributed by the owner from the steward who had buried his coin: a zero rate of return.

Jesus used a parable about money as a way to get the main point across: *increasing your productivity is an ethical requirement.* It is also a judicial requirement. The best way to increase someone's productivity is to make him an owner. God then holds him responsible. In the parable, God did not hand over ownership to a committee. He handed it over to individuals.

2. Window

Wealth serves as a tool of production. In the case of Samuel's warning, the focus was on the output of the land and the household: seeds, domesticated animals, and servants. Some of these assets served as consumption goods. But they could also be converted into production goods: capital. It is clear from the parable of the talents that God expects a positive rate of return on His investments. This means that owners must set aside a portion of their wealth for investment purposes.

The free market allows owners to increase their wealth by serving customers. Asset owners—customers—bid against each other for the output of capital. They are the strongest bidders for assets. They own money. *Money is the most marketable commodity.* The capital owner then decides whose bid to accept, including his own if he decides not to sell. He can select from a wide range of bidders. If he is successful in producing goods and services desirable in the eyes of customers, he then allocates his output by the rule of every auction among strangers: *high bid wins.*

This allows resource owners to bid for ownership or temporary control over each other's assets. Owners of money (buyers) compete against each other. Owners of goods (sellers) compete against each other. Out of this competition comes an array of prices. The highest bidder wins, product by product, auction by auction. This *judicial system of voluntary resource allocation* allows people with any amount of wealth to seek to exchange whatever they own for whatever they would like to own. This is a judicial system of liberty. It produces an economic system of exchange. What is being exchanged? Ownership: legal immunities and economic stewardship.

In the free market system, the most efficient—least wasteful—producers gain an increasing share of the society's wealth. As long as they continue meet the demands of competing customers, they will continue to accumulate wealth if they are more efficient than their competitors. Meanwhile, those producers who are not efficient in meeting the demands of customers will be losers. They will steadily experience a depletion of their capital. Capital is transferred, through voluntary competition, from inefficient producers to efficient producers. The arbitrators of this transfer are customers, who reward the most efficient producers. This system of ownership encourages capital owners to continue to produce. It leads to capital accumulation: better tools. It leads to richer customers: higher output/income and more choices. This ownership system hands control over the scarce means of production to customers by way of their economic agents: efficient producers. Customers retain authority in this auction process because they own money: the most marketable commodity.

3. Stone

In this case, the stone is a tax increase. There is no easy way to disguise a new tax as a benefit to the nation or the taxpayer. It is usually seen for what it is: a liability. People are rarely persuaded when a Keynesian economist says: "A tax hike will create jobs." This is job-creation for tax collectors. This does not impress voters. In this case, "the thing not seen" is clearly seen. A spoonful of Keynesian sugar does not make the medicine go down.

The way for politicians to sell a tax increase to a majority of voters is to persuade middle-class voters that only the rich will pay the new tax. Middle-class voters keep buying this obvious lie. They are told that there is too much economic inequality today. They think the rich can afford to pay. The following question never seems to occur to American voters: "If the rich have not been paying their fair share of taxes ever since 1914, maybe the latest tax hike proposal will not be paid by them, either." Jealousy prevails. They accept the new tax. But even if they do not pay it out of their bank accounts, they will still pay, as we shall see.

The state collects a portion of the money of existing property owners. The ownership of money is transferred from owners who are responsible before God, and who are inescapably the economic agents of money-bidding customers, into the hands of bureaucrats, who are agents of the state. The bureaucrats, who are under the general rule of the central government, then use the newly confiscated money as a way to satisfy the various competitors for the state's wealth. The politicians have already authorized the tax code. The bureaucrats now collect the money and hand it out.

In a democratic system, there are many bidders for the state's newly confiscated assets. They bid in political currency: votes. They also bid in the form of contributions to political campaigners. They may even bid in the form of under-the-table payoffs to specific legislators. Exchanges take place. Politicians decide how much they have to pay to politically adept special-interest groups.

In every division-of-labor economy, there is specialization. Politics is no exception. Special-interest groups specialize in obtaining special favors for their members. Potential recipients of government largesse specialize in how to get their hands on the state's confiscated wealth. In contrast, the voters, not having enough time or interest to study exactly what is done with the money confiscated from them individually, pay far less attention to the details of the state's voluminous wealth transfers. The public tries to compete with these specialists by voting every few years, but they are not as skilled in retaining their wealth as the special-interest groups are skilled in obtaining the voters' wealth. The only way voters can compete is by refusing to vote for politicians who vote to raise taxes. This is the specialty of voting *no*. Few politicians ever develop this skill. They are too busy buying votes with confiscated money. So, the field of available candidates is severely limited.

The primary difference between the competitive free market and the state is this: *there is no legalized coercion in the competitive free market.* Owners have a legal right to reject bids. In contrast, when an agent of the civil government comes calling, taxpayers do not have the right to reject what is now the highest bid. This bid is enforced by a gun. Someone with a badge has a gun, and he is in a position to collect the government's declared share of the asset owner's wealth.

The asset owner has a direct incentive not to waste his wealth. The bureaucratic agencies that redistribute wealth do not take the same degree of interest in allocating wealth in a way that will increase future production. The stone breaks the window of wealth creation.

4. Costs

Because of the transfer of asset ownership from individual owners to bureaucratic agencies operating under the general jurisdiction of politicians, the economy's emphasis steadily shifts from increasing the capital base by means of satisfying customer demand to decreasing the capital base by satisfying special-interest demand for "free" money.

Special-interest groups do not pay a market price in direct competition with the general public. They pay a non-market price to politicians in order to receive a net increase by means of the state's confiscated wealth. If they are successful in their political bidding, they will have more wealth at the end of the redistribution process than they had before it began. The taxpayers will have less wealth.

The focus of the individual owner who wishes to increase his wealth is on saving, accurate forecasting, efficient production, and the reinvestment of profits. The corporate focus of a bureaucracy is to get a larger budget in the following fiscal year. This money is supplied by the legislature. The bureaucracy's other major goal is to increase its overall jurisdiction. When bureaucracies are successful in this two-fold quest, the result is an increase in the amount of wealth transferred to bureaucracies and therefore a decrease in the rate of economic growth. The money is transferred from people who have an incentive to invest their personal wealth to another group of people who have an incentive to spend the state's wealth. The bureaucrats cannot lay personal claim to a share of this confiscated wealth as individuals, but they receive lifetime career salaries for distributing it.

Owners specialize in increasing production. Bureaucrats specialize in decreasing production. So, the cost of the modern tax system is a decrease of production. Specialists in distributing wealth by means of coercion gain greater control over the capital base of the society. This is the division of labor in action, as established through state coercion.

Producers have a long-term view of capital growth because they or their families will be the beneficiaries of this growth. Politicians have a short-term view of taxation and spending—a view which does not extend beyond the next election. So, the tax system transfers decision-making from people who have a long-term commitment to capital formation and increasing productivity to people who have a short-term commitment to winning the next election.

A tax on the guy behind the tree will reduce the wealth of other citizens. He had more productive uses for his money than paying taxes, but now he will not be spending money his way. He will at some point lose interest in working for the state. He will stop taking so many risks with his money. He knows the rule: "Win, and the state wins with me. Lose, and I lose alone."

5. Consequences

The consequences of raising taxes should be obvious. Production slows because capital is transferred from specialists in production to specialists in political distribution. The salaried, job-protected specialists in transferring confiscated wealth do not conserve scarce resources, let alone increase them. They have this attitude: "There is always more where that came from." This is because they possess the legal authority to extract wealth from productive members of the society. Voters grant them this authority.

The social order pays a price. First, it loses liberty because wealth is transferred to an agency of coercion. Second, there is reduced productivity because capital is transferred to those who do not invest their own money, but who transfer this money to special-interest groups that are successful in political bidding.

People who are successful in building wealth then devote less of their wealth to capital formation than they would otherwise have done. Why? Because the results of their efforts and their investments in a market ruled by uncertainty, if successful, will be taxed. The political oligarchs who are skilled in gaining money through political pressuring increase their authority in the social order.

Customers then will have reduced choices available to them because economic output has been reduced by the tax system. For as long as most of them vote for politicians who vote to raise taxes, or merely to keep taxes where they are, they will continue to disinherit themselves.

Conclusions

When taxes increase, the rate of growth of personal wealth decreases. The rate of wealth creation decreases because customers have a reduced range of choices available to them. They might have increased their savings as a result of the greater range of choices, but there is no greater range of choices. The state confiscated their money.

It is difficult to persuade voters that taxation is reducing the rate of economic growth. Why? Because there has been incomparable economic growth in the world as a whole. From approximately 1800 until the present, the only decade in which there was not steady economic growth in the West was the decade of the Great Depression: the 1930's. People do not understand economic cause-and-effect. They also do not understand this moral principle: "Thou shalt not steal, even by majority vote." So, they continue to vote for programs of state wealth redistribution, always in the hope that the rich will at long last pay a greater percentage of their income than the common taxpayer pays. But the state is never content to tax only the rich. The state wants every productive citizen to pay his fair share, which always means more.

People's voting behavior will not change until such time as they are trapped by national government debt that has been incurred in the name of predictable tax receipts. But tax receipts will not be sufficient to meet the state's legal obligations. The state will not be able to borrow at low interest rates any longer. Hyperinflation will not work, because the state has made long-term promises, and hyperinflation can last only a few years before the currency is destroyed. But the political promises still remain in the law books.

Voters are very much like the people of Israel in the days of Samuel. They do not listen to the argument that the state will confiscate a large portion of their wealth. They always think that they will be winners in the political wealth redistribution process. They become the losers, for they do not specialize in between elections. The winners are specialists in tax avoidance and wealth redistribution: large corporations and industries that hire highly skilled lawyers, accountants, and lobbyists. A voter cannot affect the outcome of an election. A lobbyist can affect the wording of one paragraph in a 1,000-page tax bill. Who benefits most from political specialization?

There are three ways by which voters may someday come to their senses. The first is a moral transformation. They may finally decide not to steal by means of the voting booth. Second, they may finally figure out the economic argument that they are made poorer by the tax system. Third, and far more likely, they will learn their lesson, just as the Hebrews learned their lesson under King Rehoboam, when tax increases bring widespread pain to all of those who have become dependent upon the state's wealth-transfer process. When the non-market auction for votes at last undermines the economy, voters may finally decide to rely on the free market's auction process: gaining ownership of other people's assets by means of voluntary exchange, not coercion. They may at last abandon this commandment: "Thou shalt not steal, except by majority vote."

Further Reading

For support material, go to bit.ly/CEIOL-Doc-5.

6

Credit Diverts Production

He that is surety for a stranger shall smart for it: and he that hateth suretiship is sure (Proverbs 11:15).

The older term, *surety*, is not widely used today. The term today is this: *co-sign*. The warning is still as valid today as it was in the days of Solomon. Do not co-sign a note for a stranger. But Solomon went beyond this. He recommended that nobody co-sign a note for a friend, either (Prov. 6:1–5).

When you co-sign a note, you become the collateral for a loan. A lender has decided that the person who requests a loan has insufficient collateral. The borrower has no way to pay back the loan, should his plans for the borrowed money go awry. He has insufficient marketable assets in reserve. In other words, *he has a low credit rating*. The lender does not want to make the loan on this basis. So, the prospective borrower seeks out somebody who does have collateral, and who does have a good credit rating. He asks this person to co-sign the loan. So, if he defaults on the loan, the creditor will then come to the solvent friend of the now-insolvent debtor. He will collect the money owed to him from the solvent friend.

Solomon recommended that nobody co-sign a note for a friend. Obviously, if it is a bad idea to co-sign a note for friend, it is an even worse idea to co-sign for a stranger.

It should be clear from this pair of proverbs that credit diverts production. Productive capital is shifted from one investment to another investment. The would-be borrower did not have sufficient credit to warrant this shift of investment.

Only after his solvent friend co-signed the note was the creditor willing to divert production, meaning capital assets used in production, from his previously highest-ranked investment opportunity to the new one. He would not have diverted his capital, had the solvent individual not been willing to co-sign the note. The signature of the friend lowered the risk of default for the creditor. This moved the loan into first place on the creditor's scale of investment opportunities.

With this in mind, let us consider the economics of government loans to businesses.

1. Owners

Who are the owners, and what do they own?

There are two owners: the lender and the borrower. The lender owns money. This is a capital asset. It could be used for consumption purposes, but the owner is a capitalist. He prefers to put his money to use in order to gain even more money later on. He looks for borrowers with good credit ratings to lend to. Because the lender owns money, what he owns is easy to see and understand. What is not easy to see or understand is what the borrower owns: credit worthiness (at some rate of interest). This is the thing not seen. Henry Hazlitt put it this way:

> There is a strange idea abroad, held by all monetary cranks, that credit is something a banker gives to a man. Credit, on the contrary, is something a man already has. He has it, perhaps, because he already has marketable assets of a greater cash value than the loan for which he is asking. Or he has it because his character and past record have earned it. He brings it into the bank with him. That is why the banker makes him the loan. The banker is not giving something for nothing. He feels assured of repayment. He is merely exchanging a more liquid form of asset or credit for a less liquid form. Sometimes he makes a mistake, and then it is not

only the banker who suffers, but the whole community; for values which were supposed to be produced by the lender are not produced and resources are wasted.

In any economic transaction, there is an exchange. The exchange is *an exchange of ownership*, either permanently or temporarily. In this case, it is a temporary exchange of ownership. The owner of money lends money, meaning the use of money, to a borrower. What does he receive in exchange? He receives a promise of repayment of the original loan, plus an additional payment, later on. The rate of interest—the price of the loan—is in the contract. So is the length of the loan: the deadline for repayment.

The lender knows better than to seek something for nothing. So, what does he seek? He seeks a written promise of repayment. He seeks it from someone who possesses good credit. The borrower's credit rating is the asset that undergirds the written promise to repay. Therefore, the borrower is someone with capital. This capital is his reputation as a reliable participant in the economy.

Because both of the participants in the exchange are owners of capital, this makes an exchange economically rational for both of them. Because each of them is an owner, each of them has legal sovereignty to make the exchange. Each of them possesses ownership rights in his respective forms of capital. Property rights mean immunity from coercion, either by private citizens or by the state. The threat is this: the state may revoke some or all of these ownership rights.

2. Window

Because each of the participants has the right to make an exchange, each of them can act to achieve his goals. Each of them seeks to improve his situation. The owner of money wants more money in the future. The owner of good credit has some use for the money during a specified period of time. He therefore borrows the money, using it in whatever way he chooses, on this basis: he will repay the creditor in the future. This enables a borrower to buy either consumer goods or production goods. He is able to use this money to achieve his goals. He then makes bids on assets.

If he is a capitalist, he buys capital equipment, raw materials, labor services, and perhaps land where he can operate a business. He does so in the hope that he will be able to produce a product or service that will be valuable to customers in the future. He thinks they will be willing to pay him more than he has paid to buy or rent the goods and services necessary to produce consumer goods or services. In other words, he buys low and sells high. The loan that he receives from the capitalist enables him better to serve the demands of future customers. If he is correct in his plans, he will reap a profit, and he will then repay the loan with interest. The lender gets what he wants. The borrower gets what he wants. Customers get what they want. The original investment leads to greater production, which in turn leads to greater customer satisfaction.

In each case, the asset owner acts on behalf of future customers, i.e., money owners. Each asset owner is a representative, economically speaking, of these future customers. Of course, these future customers may decide to become future non-customers. They retain the legal right not to purchase goods and services. But, from an economic standpoint, the capitalists must operate as representative agents for future customers. Because customers have money, and money is the most marketable commodity, customers are in authority.

3. Stone

Into this voluntary series of voluntary arrangements comes the state. The state taxes individuals and businesses in order to gain revenue. It also borrows money from lenders. In some cases, it borrows money from central banks, which create new money out of nothing in order to buy IOU's from the government.

An agency of the state then makes money available to businesses. It makes loans at a rate of interest that is lower than what the borrower would have to pay in the private capital markets. There is a reason why the borrower would have to pay more in the private capital markets: he has a low credit rating. This is another way of saying that he is a higher risk borrower than other borrowers in the market for loans. Bankers and other potential lenders have examined this person's past credit, and they have determined that this person is a bad credit risk at a low rate of interest. In order to make a loan viable, he must pay a higher rate of interest, in order to compensate the lenders for the higher risk of dealing with him. He then goes shopping for a loan from the government.

An agency of the state then determines that this borrower deserves a loan. The state takes some of the money that it has confiscated from taxpayers, and it turns this money over to the borrower. It does so at a below-market rate of interest. Private lenders would have charged the borrower more, given his low credit rating.

The state agency does this for a reason. Such loans are popular with voters. Also, the state agency does not put its own money at risk. It will get more money in the next fiscal year. It has a guaranteed source of money for as long as the politicians decide that it is good politics to fund the agency with more confiscated money. In other words, the agency does not make the determination based on economics; it makes the determination based on politics.

4. Costs

We never get something for nothing. Therefore, we should follow the money. We should search for the things not seen.

Here is what is not seen by the general public. First, money that would otherwise have been available to professional lenders to lend to borrowers with high credit ratings is not available to the lenders, because it has been confiscated by the state. Second, those borrowers who would have obtained loans, based on their high credit ratings, are not able to obtain these loans, because the money has been funneled from the government tax-collecting agency to the agency that makes loans available to high-risk borrowers at below-market interest rates.

Then there are the future customers of those borrowers who would have used the borrowed money to go into production. They do not go into production, because they did not gain access to a loan. Because there was less money available to private lenders, because the government had confiscated the money, the lenders are not in a position to lend out money to otherwise qualified borrowers. The future customers of these borrowers pay the price. They do not perceive that they pay a price, because they do not see the goods or services that are not offered to them for sale. These are things not seen.

Because the borrowers are higher-risk borrowers, there is a higher rate of default on these loans. Who makes payment on these defaulted loans? Who has co-signed the notes? The taxpayers. They do not know that they have co-signed the notes, but they have. The government agency that lent the money, which was confiscated from the taxpaying public, does not pursue the now-bankrupt borrowers. They write off the loans. This is wasted capital. But then, sure as clockwork, the agency has these lost funds replenished by politicians in the next fiscal year. The losers are the taxpayers. The lending agencies co-signed the notes on behalf of the taxpayers, but without the knowledge of the taxpayers. The taxpayers pay the agencies in the next fiscal year.

Because customers face a reduced range of choices for their money, they are poorer. They do not perceive that they are poorer, because they do not see the things not seen: the goods and services that would otherwise have been offered to them, but which were not produced, precisely because the government had extracted wealth from potential lenders, and because the government then loaned the confiscated money to producers without experience, and without good credit, but who qualified in terms of political criteria rather than economic criteria. They were the right sort of borrowers from a political standpoint.

Some customers are benefited, of course. These are the customers of the companies that did not go bankrupt after they borrowed money from the government agency. These customers have their wants satisfied, but had the government not confiscated the money from the taxpayers, these customers would have had to pay more for whatever it is they wanted to buy. This is because there would have been fewer goods and services offered to them. The entrepreneurs and capitalists who would have borrowed the money in the private markets, but who could not do so, would have produced a different set of products and services. They would have served other customers.

So, there is a redistribution of wealth between certain classes of customers. This is not perceived by the customers, nor is it perceived by the politicians, but this is the inevitable outcome of the initial intervention into the market by the state. It leads to reduced production, and it also leads to the subsidizing of certain groups of customers. These customers are subsidized by those customers who did not find the goods and services they wanted at prices they were willing to pay, because of the original intervention into the marketplace

5. Consequences

The result of the intervention, as always, is reduced economic growth. Those producers in the marketplace who have good credit ratings, and who were willing and able to borrow money from lenders, do not get access to the money they need in order to go into production. This reduces production.

At the same time, those borrowers who qualified politically for the loans from the government did go into production, but because they were higher credit risks, the rate of default exceeded those rates of default common among private lenders. This capital is wasted. It is not lent out by the government agency the next year, because it never comes back to the government agency. Instead, the borrower defaulted on the loan.

Government-supplied credit diverts production from high-output producers, who would otherwise have met the demands of customers. It shifts production to high-risk producers. This subsidizes the customers of those high-risk producers who do not go out of business and default on their loans. In other words, capital is shifted by government intervention from high-output, low-risk producers to lower-output, higher-risk producers. This leads to reduced production. It leads to reduced rates of economic growth. It leads to a reduced supply of capital. It therefore leads to reduced per capita wealth in the society.

Conclusions

The existence of various kinds of subsidies to businesses, especially export-oriented businesses, is an old story. It goes back to mercantilism in the 16th century. Adam Smith did his best to refute the errors of mercantilism in 1776, but the errors still persist.

Generally, the big money in credit diversion is associated with big businesses. But the justification politically always is the help that government loans give to small businesses. This is comparable to the justification of farm subsidies. The overwhelming percentage of the farm subsidies go to large-scale agribusiness organizations, but the justification is always in favor of saving small farmers, who constitute about 2% of the American population. Big businesses are much better at lobbying than small businesses are. They have more money to spend.

The voters hear about loans to small businesses, so they accept the idea of government loans to small businesses. This provides the political cover. The thing not seen politically is this: most of the money flows to big businesses.

The government becomes the literal co-signer of the notes, so big businesses then borrow on the credit of the national government. The lenders benefit, because they have what they believe to be a solvent co-signer of the notes. Big banks, big businesses, and big government siphon off money from the general public, and the agency of this confiscation does so by co-signing the notes.

Solomon knew better.

Further Reading

For supporting material, go to bit.ly/CEIOL-Doc-6.

–7–

The Curse of Machinery

And Pharaoh commanded the same day the taskmas-
ters of the people, and their officers, saying, Ye shall no
more give the people straw to make brick, as heretofore:
let them go and gather straw for themselves. And the
tale of the bricks, which they did make heretofore, ye
shall lay upon them; ye shall not diminish ought there-
of: for they be idle; therefore they cry, saying, Let us go
and sacrifice to our God. Let there more work be laid
upon the men, that they may labour therein; and let
them not regard vain words (Exodus 5:6–9).

Three issues were involved here: theological, judicial, and
economic. Theologically, it was this question: "Who is
God: the gods of Egypt or the God of Moses?" Judicially, it was
this question: "Who represented God in history, Pharaoh or
Moses?" Economically, it was this question: "Does a decrease
in the division of labor make men poorer?"

According to the polytheistic theology of Egypt, Pharaoh
was a god. He was the primary link between the realm of the
gods and mankind. The Egyptian state was therefore divine.
Pharaoh was the pinnacle at the top of this pyramid of earthly
power. Moses was calling this theology into question. Pharaoh
recognized this. "And Pharaoh said, Who is the LORD, that I
should obey his voice to let Israel go? I know not the LORD,
neither will I let Israel go" (v. 2).

Moses at this point in the confrontation was not calling for
the exodus. He was demanding—not asking—that the He-

69

brews be permitted to journey three days from their compulsory work center, participate in a covenantal feast, and then return. Pharaoh recognized that this was an attack on his divinity and therefore also on the legitimacy of the Egyptian state. This would be a festival of liberation. He refused to let them go. This was the beginning of the public confrontation between two cultures. One was thoroughly statist. The other was not.

Pharaoh imposed negative sanctions on the Hebrews, but not on Moses. He sought to undermine Moses in the eyes of the people. The punishment was economic: Pharaoh's refusal to supply the Hebrew slaves with straw. Straw was a necessary ingredient in bricks. This new rule forced onto the slaves an additional task: gathering straw. This decreased the division of labor. It increased the costs of production. It therefore increased the workload on the slaves. That was the goal of the decree. Pharaoh understood basic economics.

What if some inventor after this declaration had come up with a way to increase the output of straw gatherers? What if he invented a reaper that cut down the straw faster? Would this piece of machinery have increased the division of labor for the Hebrews? Of course. Would this have decreased the slaves' workload? Of course. Would this have been a benefit to the slaves? Of course. Would Pharaoh have outlawed the Hebrews' use of this invention? Of course.

A problem that we face today is this: modern politicians imitate Pharaoh. They adopt a comparable policy of restricting the introduction of tools that increase the division of labor and thereby increase the productivity of workers. They do so for the same reason that Pharaoh did: to increase the amount of labor necessary to complete required tasks. What is different is this: they justify this as a humanitarian measure. Pharaoh knew better. He was a far better economist than the typical politician is today.

Let us consider the economics of the hatred of labor-saving machinery.

1. Owners

Who are the owners, and what do they own?

There are multiple owners: an inventor with an idea, a customer with money to spend, a capitalist with money to invest, a businessman with organizational abilities and also an assessment of the economic future, an owner of raw materials or land, and a worker with labor to sell. Each of them is legally sovereign over whatever asset he owns. He possesses the legal right to exclude others—the essence of ownership. Each of them wants to benefit from his property. Each of them needs the cooperation of the others. They have the potential for increasing their wealth through cooperation.

They all benefit from a private property legal order. This means that the free market itself is an economic asset. The legal rights of property are assets. But these assets are legally different from the other forms of property. They cannot be bought and sold on an open market.

Consider workers, since the loss of jobs is the focus of the resentment against machinery. Workers own the right to rent their labor services. Some new technique of production may or may not lead to greater income for all of them. If they become skilled in using the new machine, they will benefit from rising wages. But they may be dismissed from employment if the cost of the marginal output of the machine costs less than hiring a particular laborer. The machine in no way interferes with the legal right of workers to make bids to employers. They do not own their jobs; they own only the right to make a bid for a job. *Nobody owns a job.* A job is the outcome of successful mutual bids: employers vs. employers, and workers vs. workers.

Workers are not the only owners involved in the introduction of new machinery. All owners may be affected. But the legal and moral issue at hand is the right of all owners to make bids.

2. Window

The business owner, the inventor of the new machine, the resource owner, the capital owner, and the worker all act as economic agents of future customers. The customers retain authority, because they possess the most marketable commodity: money. Their decisions in the future will determine which businesses, which inventors, and which workers were correct in assessing the future demand of customers.

The system of economic sanctions in a free market economy mandates that producers serve the demands of customers. So, from the point of view of customers, it is irrelevant whether a machine or a human being has produced what they want to buy. The customers want the best possible deal. If the introduction of machinery leads to a decrease in employment for certain workers, customers are probably unaware of it, and even if they are aware of it, most of them do not care. What they care about is themselves. In this respect, they are no different from the businessman who decides to buy the labor-saving machine, the inventor who sells the machine, and the workers who will use the machines in order to increase their personal output and thereby keep their jobs.

If the labor-saving machine or process decreases the cost of labor for business, then in all likelihood the businessman will decide to increase total output, in order to sell this output to a greater number of customers. In order to sell to more customers, the business will have to lower the prices of the final products. This is a benefit for customers, although it will not be a benefit to rival businesses, rival workers, and rival sellers of machinery. But the free market system is not structured so as to benefit producers at the expense of customers; it is an outcome of a private property system which inherently benefits customers. Customers shout: "May the best man win—as determined by us."

3. Stone

The stone is thrown at machines. Politicians do this in the name of protecting existing jobs. The politicians ignore customers. They ignore future jobs. These are things not seen by politicians. "Workers own jobs!" But they do not.

Only rarely do governments ban the use of labor-saving machinery in a direct manner, i.e., by passing a law against a particular machine. Instead, governments grant monopoly authority to certain groups, and these groups are then able to restrict the introduction of new labor-saving equipment, except on terms amenable to the groups.

If a new production technique involves new machines, then it may receive considerable criticism, especially from members of labor unions. Labor unions enjoy special privileges that are granted by the government. When a labor union receives a majority vote among the existing employees of a business to represent all of the workers from that point on, the government does not allow the business to fire employees and then go into the marketplace to hire replacements. This is a grant of monopoly privilege. So, the business may hesitate to introduce new machines. It does not want workers to go out on strike. The workers may oppose the introduction of the machine unless the employer guarantees that there will be no layoffs in response to the increased productivity of the new machine. This makes it more expensive for the employer to put the new machine into production.

Governments often do not introduce new machinery or techniques in order to increase their own productivity. Their employees resist such introductions. This is an advantage for the private sector, because the private sector can and does introduce new production techniques, and these tend to escape the regulatory structure of the governments. Government regulatory agencies play catch-up to new technologies in the private sector all the time.

One way to counter the hostility against the introduction of new machinery is to ask the critic this question: "Would it be wise to ban the use of shovels and mandate the use of spoons for building new highways?" No? "Would it be wise to ban the use of bulldozers, and then hire more workers to use only shovels?" No? "Then what is the case for banning new machinery?"

The stone also disrupts the legal system of ownership. The threat to private ownership represented by the intervention reduces the wealth of all participants. The value of private property falls, because the cost of defending it against the state rises.

4. Costs

Whenever government regulations restrict the introduction of new machinery or new techniques of production, this violates the ownership rights of business owners, inventors, and customers, who then have to pay higher prices for whatever it is that they buy, when they might have benefitted from lower prices as a result of the introduction of new machinery.

There is the basic cost of all government interference, namely, a violation of ownership rights. This is resented by the victims. This cost should never be ignored. It is usually ignored, and when it is not ignored, it is dismissed as an apology for the rich. In any case, it is clearly a denial of the rule of law. That is also a cost of operation.

It is true that some workers may not lose their jobs as a result of the prohibition of the introduction of new machinery. But that only applies briefly. Rival companies then have an opportunity to buy the machine and begin production. The other firms are able to undercut the prices of goods and services offered by the firms that have been prevented by the state from introducing the new machines.

If the ban is national, then foreign businesses will be able to buy the machine, increase production, and undercut the prices of the domestic manufacturers, who had been prohibited from introducing the new technique or new machine. Competition is international. Stones thrown inside a nation's borders weaken the competitiveness of domestic workers and business owners. Then the employees of these businesses will lose their jobs anyway, because the businesses will face shrinking markets. The business may even go out of business.

5. Consequences

The result of legal restrictions on the introduction of new machinery or new processes of production inevitably reduces the wealth of those customers who would have purchased the output generated by the new machines, but who refuse to buy, because prices remain high. They remain high because the new machine was not allowed to be introduced.

Customers who were able to save money would then have spent that money on other things. They might have purchased other consumer goods. They might have set the money aside to invest in production goods, which in turn led to the production of more goods and services. But this does not happen when governments restrict the introduction of labor-saving machinery.

The overall result of government bans on labor-saving equipment is to increase the cost of production and thereby decrease output. This slows the rate of economic growth for the general population. This reduces people's wealth in the long run.

Conclusion

Hostility to the introduction of labor-saving tools is concentrated among employees of specific firms that are contemplating the purchase of such equipment. The general population usually is not concerned about new labor-saving equipment. The general population really does not care how goods and services are produced.

Customers act in their own self-interest. They are always looking for better deals. They do not ask what kind of machinery made possible these deals. They do not ask how many employees were either hired or fired as a result of the introduction of these machines. In this case, the things not seen—unemployed workers—are on the side of those who favor the free market.

Over the past 250 years, governments in the West have generally not been successful in restricting the introduction of new labor-saving equipment. This is why the West has experienced such remarkable economic growth, decade after decade. Employees are focused in their concern about the introduction of such equipment, but unless they are members of labor unions, they probably are not going to be successful in persuading the government to restrict the introduction of a specific machine, in a specific industry, in a specific company. The politicians do not respond unless the workers can get out a lot of voters at the next election. Businesses in a specific industry are more likely to be able to put up large amounts of money for campaigns than the workers in that industry are.

There is another major economic factor that increases the likelihood that there will be no major restrictions on the introduction of new machinery. This is the fact that most increases of production do not come from the introduction of new machinery; they come from increases in the efficiency of computers and software. It is a lot cheaper to improve software than it is to invent, patent, produce, sell, and deploy a machine. As production moves away from manufacturing toward service industries, restrictions on the introduction of machinery become ever less relevant. There is almost no political resistance against the introduction of a specific piece of software in a specific business. This is good news.

We are told that the introduction of computerized robotics will lead to mass unemployment. There is no evidence of this so far. In any case, what can the government do about it? How can the government restrict the implementation of upgrades in software?

Further Reading

For supporting material, go to bit.ly/CEIOL-Doc-7.

Spread-the-Work Schemes

Is it not lawful for me to do what I will with mine own?
Is thine eye evil, because I am good? (Matthew 20:15).

This is the most powerful affirmation of private ownership in the New Testament. The only affirmation more authoritative was God's announcement of an ownership boundary around the forbidden tree (Genesis 2:17).

In this pair of rhetorical questions, Jesus challenged the idea that an aggrieved participant in the transaction—an early morning worker—has a moral claim retroactively against the employer, who came to an agreement with the worker, and who then fulfilled the terms of the original agreement.

The context of this affirmation of ownership rights was a parable. Jesus described a man who owned a vineyard. The owner wanted to share the work. He wanted to bring as many workers as he could into the vineyard, so that they would have employment. Of course, he also had goals of his own. He wanted to make certain that the vineyard would be cared for and made more productive. But his initial motivation was to help others gain employment.

So, one fine morning, he came to a group of unemployed laborers and made an offer. He would hire them for a day for the payment of a penny. (This was before central banking; the offer seemed plausible to Jesus' listeners.) In the third hour, which meant 9 AM, he again went out in search of other workers. He found some of them who were idle, waiting for work. He hired them, and he promised to give them an honest day's wages.

They trusted him, so they went into the vineyard to work. He did this in the sixth hour, the ninth hour, and the 11th hour. In each case, he promised to pay them fairly.

At the end of the workday, he paid each man a penny. That was what he had offered the men who had been hired early in the morning. Those who were hired later had no complaints, because they were getting paid as much for a partial day's labor as the first men who were hired received for a whole day's labor.

Those who were hired earliest complained. These others had been paid the same amount, they complained, but they had worked fewer hours. The others did not complain, although most of them did work a lot longer than the last group, who had been hired in the 11th hour, and who also received a penny. Late-comers knew that it was a good deal, because they were being paid more per hour than those who had been hired at the beginning of the workday. Why complain?

The first group did complain. The owner of the vineyard had a specific answer: "But he answered one of them, and said, Friend, I do thee no wrong: didst not thou agree with me for a penny? Take that thine is, and go thy way: I will give unto this last, even as unto thee "(vv. 13–14). Then he announced his principal ownership: he had the right to do what he wanted with that which he owned.

His goal had been to spread the work. He wanted to hire as many people as he could locate at a competitive wage. He benefitted the community, and he benefitted the individuals hired. He also benefitted himself. This was a win-win-win deal. But still, there were complaints. "It's just not fair!"

The lesson of the parable is twofold. First, the best way to spread the work is to allow voluntary negotiation. Second, *the appropriate wage is the wage that clears the market.* This means that there is nobody who wants to work who does not gain employment, and there is no employer standing around, looking for somebody to hire. Throughout the day, the employer in the parable had offered to hire all the men available at that hour. His offer cleared the market every time. Only the earliest employees complained at the end of the day.

1. Owners

In the parable, there were owners of labor to rent, and there was an owner of money to pay them. A mutually agreeable arrangement was possible. All of the labor owners got what they agreed to, hour by hour. The contract that bound them together for the day was honored by all parties.

If the owners of labor had not found a willing employer at a wage they were willing to accept, they would not have gained any money. They would also not have contributed to increased productivity to benefit specific future customers, as well as the community in general. Their skills would have been wasted in idleness. Their productivity would have been zero. This would have resulted in reduced output, which would have reduced the wealth of customers in the future. Future customers would have had a smaller array of goods to choose from.

The owner of the vineyard put his capital to good use. He had land and vines and money. By adding labor to his land, he was able to increase production. This was one of his goals. It also made possible greater income in the future, assuming that he was correct with respect to what future customers would be willing to pay for the output of his land, vines, and hired labor.

The same analysis applies to every labor contract. Someone wants to hire labor at a particular price, and he has the right to make an offer to those who might be willing to supply him with this labor at a specific price. The laborers also possess the same right of making a bid.

2. Window

A would-be employer comes to a group of possible employees. He makes an offer to them: so many hours of labor of a specific kind, in exchange for a specific amount of money.

Here is what is sometimes misunderstood. This is not a job.

This is a job *offer*. Too often, people confuse the two.

They never make this conceptual error when discussing marriage. A man may propose marriage to a woman, but this is not a marriage. There is no marriage until the two parties come together in a joint effort. The same is true of a job.

Similarly, a would-be employee may propose a job to a would-be employer. His offer to a prospective employer is just as valid legally as the would-be employer's job offer is to a group of workers. It is an offer—a bid. It may be rejected.

The legal right to bid is the source of jobs in a free society. This legal right makes possible the division of labor. Any interference by the state with the right to bid will decrease the number of legal bids. That of course is what the state's interference in the job market is all about: to decrease the number of legal bids. This law will reduce the number of jobs because it reduces the number of legal bids. Of course, I am not talking here about black market job offers. These are illegal, and they have high risks associated with them.

Then there are the would-be customers in the future. They will have money. Customers look forward today to an increasing supply of future goods and services to purchase. They dream of economic growth. The free market is a way for societies to enable customers to match their demand with supply.

3. Stone

Politicians toss a stone through the window. They do so with a political promise: there will be jobs for more workers.

First, the politicians say that there are people out there who are willing to accept job offers, but there are no job offers for them. The politicians say that this law will create jobs.

Second, politicians say that if the state forces businesses to pay higher wages per hour to any employee who works more than a standard workweek, businesses will then hire new workers at the normal weekly wage per hour. Obviously, this is a subsidy from the workers who work 40 hours a week, and who also would like to work overtime at the same hourly wage in order to earn more money. They are penalized. Their bids are declared illegal. Other workers, who have not yet worked 40 hours a week, are given the right to bid for the remaining hours of the workweek.

This is a minimum-wage law. It is rarely discussed in these terms, but that is what it is. It applies to every worker who has worked 40 hours in a week in a particular job. This time, politicians accurately assess the inevitable effect of this mini-mum-wage law: reduced employment. They understand that the law will reduce the number of jobs for a particular group of workers: workers who work 40 hours a week so far, and who want to work longer for the same wage per hour.

Politicians argue that this law will force businesses to hire part-time workers at the same hourly wage that is being paid to the 40-hour week workers. These part-time workers will be hired to do the extra work. Politicians argue that the part-time worker will be cheaper to hire for the business, which is now compelled to pay more per hour to the worker who has already worked 40 hours in the week. By raising labor costs of overtime workers, politicians say, the law will spread the work.

What about the businessman who is ready and willing to pay an existing worker if he wants to work more hours at the same hourly wage? What about the existing worker who is willing and able to work these extra hours in order to earn more mon-ey? Each of them implicitly asks this question: "Is it not lawful for me to do what I will with mine own?" The politicians who vote for this law have an answer: "No."

4. Costs

If the businessman decides to pay more per hour to a worker who works beyond the initial 40 hours a week, he will make this arrangement only with his most productive workers. Such workers are always in short supply. They are worth the extra money, and they get the extra money only because the state intervenes and makes it illegal for the businessman and other members of the workforce to work out an arrangement at the standard wage per hour.

The law raises costs for the business. Businesses then have to reduce output below what they otherwise would have produced. The only alternative is to hire part-time workers, who are obviously less efficient than full-time workers, which is why they are part-time workers. Therefore, most of the 40-hour-plus workers will not get these jobs. They will have to settle for less income.

The businessman may decide to hire part-time workers at the standard wage. But part-time workers are less productive than full-time workers who are already on the payroll. These are marginal workers. This is why no one has hired them on a full-time basis. So, in this case also, costs of production rise. Less is produced. Customers lose.

Foreign manufacturers and foreign workers can now increase their output, while keeping prices low. They become more competitive in the domestic market because they are not under a similar legal restriction against hiring full-time workers for a few hours more a week. Foreigners benefit; domestic businesses and workers do not. The law spreads the work—no question about it. It spreads the work to foreign workers. But this is not what the politicians had promised.

Because of this law, everyone in the labor markets experiences a loss of freedom, which means a reduction in the value of ownership rights of labor. This is rarely seen or mentioned in defenses of laws mandating extra pay for work beyond the normal work week. The law makes almost everyone in the society poorer. The law reduces the potential for voluntary arrangements that are mutually beneficial to employers and employees.

5. Consequences

Hazlitt in 1946 did not see what was about to begin as a result, in part, of the overtime law: the steady reduction of blue-collar jobs. First, businesses began to buy machines to do the work that blue-collar employees otherwise would have done. The machines now became profitable because the government interfered with the labor markets, which deliberately forced up the price of overtime work. Machines are not paid overtime. This reduced the amount of piece-rate work for the federal government to spread.

Second, businessmen imported partially assembled components. Workers outside the United States were able to get the jobs that domestic workers could no longer obtain because the law restricted their ability to work overtime. This reduced the amount of piece-rate work for the federal government to spread.

The third strategy of businesses was decisive. Businesses throughout the United States began to redefine blue-collar jobs as white-collar jobs. This reduced the amount of piece-rate work for the federal government to spread. Managers are paid salaries. They are not paid by the hour. So, businesses shifted production out of manufacturing and into what is known as the service sector of the economy. Salaried workers can be pressured by competition from other workers to work longer than 40 hours a week. Because white collar workers are paid a flat salary, every additional hour that they work in the payment period lowers their hourly wage rate. This is completely legal. As long as someone is not paid by the hour, the law against working overtime at the same hourly wage no longer applies.

Labor unions in the United States have had little success in organizing workers in management positions. They have had little success in organizing white collar workers generally. Because of greater political power in Western Europe, labor unions have had greater success in controlling labor markets, but in every Western nation since 1955, the percentage of output contributed to the general economy by manufacturing has fallen. It is still falling. Labor unions, with government backing, have priced blue-collar labor out of the market. The number of blue-collar jobs has steadily declined. The influence of labor unions in the general economy has also steadily declined.

Conclusion

Jesus' parable of the vineyard owner and the workers had it exactly right. The way to maximize employment is to allow sellers of labor services and buyers of labor services to work out mutually beneficial terms of employment. This process of negotiation is what allows the labor markets to clear. Workers who are willing to work at the wages offered can find employment, and employers who are willing to pay these wages can hire all the workers they want.

Christian economics has an answer to this question: "Is it not lawful for me to do what I will with mine own?" The answer of Christian economics is this: "yes."

Further Reading

For supporting material, go to bit.ly/CEIOL-Doc-8.

–9–

Disbanding Troops and Bureaucrats

And he shall judge among many people, and rebuke strong nations afar off; and they shall beat their swords into plowshares, and their spears into pruninghooks: nation shall not lift up a sword against nation, neither shall they learn war any more. But they shall sit every man under his vine and under his fig tree; and none shall make them afraid: for the mouth of the Lord of hosts hath spoken it (Micah 4:3–4).

This is a prophecy regarding "the last days" (v. 1). The description of peace—swords into ploughshares—is one of the most familiar in Western culture. It is a day that men say they dream of.

Let us assume that the day comes to pass. Can you imagine a group of economists calling for the continuation of the sword industry? They would invoke this argument: "If we get out of sword production prematurely, there will be unemployment. This would bring the post-war economy to a screeching halt. What we need is a program of sequential reduction of weapons production that does not disrupt the job market."

As for letting the troops return home, the suggestion would bring this response: "The rise in unemployment would be devastating to the post-war economy. The bulk of our troops must be kept on active duty until such time as the economy makes the transformation back to peacetime production."

How long would it take to turn swords into ploughshares under these post-war conditions? How long would the troops wait to be demobilized in order to return home? The answer would be open-ended. No one would know. Politics would decide.

If the definition of "peace" is "keeping the troops in uniform until it is clear that they can get good jobs in the private sector," then peace sounds suspiciously like preparation for the next war.

This was what the United States economy was facing in late 1945. Japan surrendered in August. Germany had surrendered the previous May. By the time that President Truman delivered his State of the Union address in January 1946, he had disbanded half of the 12 million troops who had been on active duty when Japan surrendered. In his address, he promised that most of the remainder would be demobilized by June. Hazlitt was writing this chapter about the time when Truman delivered his speech.

America's families wanted the troops disbanded. They wanted their sons and husbands out of uniform and back in the country. Truman understood this. Concerns over unemployment were not sufficient to keep him from bringing them home and demobilizing them. They came home. They hung their uniforms in a closet. Soon, they folded them, and packed them in trunks. The uniforms were mothballed. So were their owners' wartime jobs.

The troops were rapidly integrated back into the private sector. Unemployment in 1946 was low: 3.9%. It remained in this range for the remainder of the decade. Hazlitt's prediction in early 1946 was accurate:

> The soldiers previously supported by civilians will not become merely civilians supported by other civilians. They will become self-supporting civilians. If we assume that the men who would otherwise have been retained in the armed forces are no longer needed for defense, then their retention would have been sheer waste. They would have been unproductive. The taxpayers, in return for supporting them, would have got

nothing. But now the taxpayers turn over this part of their funds to them as fellow civilians in return for equivalent goods or services. Total national production, the wealth of everybody, is higher.

But what about wartime bureaucrats? Here was the question: "Can the private sector absorb them?" Hazlitt said it would. Here was a second question: "Is it a good idea to dismiss them?" Hazlitt argued that it was a good idea.

But the vast majority of these employees remained on the payroll. In fact, more were hired, year by year. The argument that almost everyone applied to the troops was not applied to the wartime bureaucrats: "Bring the boys home. Let them get on with their lives." The politicians, the bureaucrats, and the voters concluded that the logic that applied to men in uniform did not apply to non-combatant bureaucrats who had not gone off to war.

With this as background, let us consider the economics of keeping wartime bureaucrats on the federal government's payroll.

1. Owners

War is a matter of coercion. It is a non-market phenomenon. Ludwig von Mises wrote this in 1944: "History has witnessed the failure of many endeavors to impose peace by war, coöperation by coercion, unanimity by slaughtering dissidents."

Before a war begins, citizens are owners. Their primary asset is their lives. They are stewards of their lives under God.

Except for a handful of government employees, citizens earn their livings through voluntary exchange. They have jobs. They do not own their jobs. Jobs are temporary products of competitive bidding. But the bidders own the skills they possess. In a free market social order, they own the right to make bids to others. They buy and sell. Among the things that they buy and sell are employment skills.

They also own that portion of their income that is not extracted by taxes, including the losses imposed by monetary inflation and government regulations of the economy.

2. Window

Unlike the other chapters in Hazlitt's book, the window here is pre-war. The window is peace. It is the right of people to make voluntary arrangements with each other in order to attain their goals as owners of their lives, talents, and money.

In peacetime, individuals decide where to work and at what compensation. Employers compete against employers. Employees compete against employees. Out of this competition comes an array of wages. At some price, a labor market clears: no unemployed people willing to work at that wage, and no employers unable to hire workers at this wage.

This is not the case in wartime.

3. Stone

The stone is the war. Civil governments seek to impose coercion on foreign citizens and also on domestic citizens. This disrupts citizens' pre-war priorities. It therefore disrupts pre-war labor markets.

During the war, voters consent to higher levels of taxation, government borrowing, and central bank monetary inflation. They also consent to price and wage controls.

The labor markets adjust to the new conditions of the supply and demand for labor. This adjustment is invariably administered by bureaucrats, who impose price and wage ceilings. The phrase "price and wage controls" really means this: *people controls*. The state's bureaucrats threaten violence against people who buy or sell at prices above the legal maximums. This intervention always produces shortages. The government then introduces non-price rationing. This system of the mobilization of labor may also be accompanied by military conscription: the draft. The labor markets during wartime are not free markets. *State coercion is basic to clearing the labor markets in wartime.* This domestic coercion is justified by invoking the war. This is said to be the price of victory. This was the universal phrase in the United States in response to shortages: "Don't you know there's a war on?"

Here is the economic question raised in this chapter: "Should the national civil government stop throwing stones into the labor markets after the war is over?" In the market for military service, the state is likely to reduce the number and size of these stones. But this is not true of the labor market for wartime bureaucrats. The politicians offer new justifications for keeping wartime bureaucrats on the payroll.

Men who were forced by the threat of violence to join the armed forces—conscription—did not own their jobs. They probably did not want these jobs. They had refused to volunteer, so they were drafted. Most men in World War II were drafted into the armed services. But some volunteered. The threat of conscription always backed up the system of volunteering.

In contrast, wartime bureaucrats were all volunteers. They remained safely stateside. Most bureaucrats remain stateside in every war. There is no organization known as the BFW: Bureaucrats of Foreign Wars.

The legal justification for the massive shift away from pre-war employment patterns is based on the moral foundation of the war. When the war ends, the moral justification for the continuation of these jobs also ends. The surviving owners of their lives are allowed by the state to reclaim possession. The national government demobilizes the troops.

In contrast, stateside bureaucrats are reassigned to new positions, or at least newly defined positions. The moral and legal justifications for their original employment disappear. An economic justification is substituted: "If we fire them, they will stop spending. This will depress the economy." This is a Keynesian argument.

Taxpayers must therefore continue to be taxed in order to keep these bureaucrats on the payroll. Their ownership of their income is reduced by taxes.

President Truman did disband the armed forces. He also cut the number of civilian employees by over half within two years. There were about 3.4 million civilian employees of the U.S. government in 1945. This was cut to 2.2 million in 1946. It was down to 1.6 million in 1947. It bottomed in 1950 at 1.4 million. It went back up to 2 million in the Korean War. The government conceals the vast army of employees who are hired as subcontractors in the private sector.

4. Costs

Some of the costs of the war decline when the war ends. Conscription ends for most men. Taxes may go down. Central bank inflation may end. Price and wage controls may end.

In the case of wartime bureaucrats, their salaries continue to be paid. Because their wartime assignments ended with the war, new assignments are discovered or invented. The federal government continues to tax, borrow, and spend. Money that would otherwise have remained in the possession of peacetime taxpayers and investors continues to be transferred to the federal government. This money is used to keep bureaucrats on the payroll.

We are back once again to Bastiat's contrast between the things seen and the things not seen—the heart of Hazlitt's analysis. The bureaucrats are seen. The goods and services that they buy are seen. What is not seen are the goods and services that would have been bought by taxpayers, had the bureaucrats been fired and their salaries eliminated. The taxpayers now do not buy these things. Producers who would have supplied these things now do not hire workers to produce these goods and services. Investors who would otherwise have provided the capital for such ventures decide instead to buy government bonds. Hazlitt described this outcome:

> Once again the fallacy comes from looking at the effects of this action only on the dismissed officeholders themselves and on the particular tradesmen who

depend upon them. Once again it is forgotten that, if these bureaucrats are not retained in office, the tax-payers will be permitted to keep the money that was formerly taken from them for the support of the bureaucrats. Once again it is forgotten that the taxpayers' income and purchasing power go up by at least as much as the income and purchasing power of the former officeholders go down.

Had they returned to the private sector, the bureaucrats would have become productive citizens—as determined by customers. The work that the bureaucrats had performed during the war was justified politically in the name of military victory. But after the war, taxpayers are no longer willing to suffer taxes in the name of national wartime sacrifice. They want to pursue their own affairs. How, under these circumstances, can they be persuaded to hand over money to the government to pay salaries to post-war bureaucrats?

If wartime bureaucrats stay on the government's payroll, taxpayers must forego some of their post-war goals. This is the cost of keeping bureaucrats on the payroll. To hide this cost, Keynesian economists came up with this argument: "If the federal government keeps them on the payroll, they will spend money. This will stimulate the economy. Taxpayers will be better off than if the bureaucrats are fired and their jobs get mothballed." Hazlitt wrote this in response: "When we can find no better argument for the retention of any group of officeholders than that of retaining their purchasing power, it is a sign that the time has come to get rid of them."

5. Consequences

Post-war West Germany and Japan experienced unprecedented economic booms after 1949. Their wartime controls ended. Free markets were substituted for the pre-war and wartime economic regulations. These two nations were not allowed to re-arm. So, their populations were spared the fiscal burden of the military. This was especially true of Japan. These booms constituted the "peace dividend" of a foreign military-imposed anti-militarism. This exemption from militarism enabled both economies to become economic powerhouses after 1949. Their export-oriented businesses became formidable economic competitors to the military victors of World War II.

Conclusions

Wartime economic controls in the United States ended in late 1946. They did not end in Great Britain. The British had to suffer price and wage controls and rationing until the Labor government was defeated in late 1951.

The justification of conscription and wartime economic controls is the war itself. When the war ends, the justification should end. But bureaucracy in the twentieth century became a way of life. It expanded as it had not done ever since the days of the Pharaohs.

There were 700,000 civilian federal employees in 1940. It has never fallen below 1.4 million. Contract civilian workers are in fact on the government payroll. This is concealed statistically.

Once the state spends money to hire bureaucrats, politicians can frighten voters into maintaining the existing staffs. Politicians use this argument: "Government employment reduces national unemployment." The politicians do not believe that the free market will adjust wages, so that everyone who wants employment at a market wage will receive a job offer. Keynesian economists echo this view. The voters shrug, and then pay the taxes to keep bureaucrats on the payrolls. The things unseen remain unseen. This includes the reduced wealth of most taxpayers . . . but not the bureaucrats.

American voters in 1946 would no longer tolerate wartime spending. In the November elections, Republicans took back both houses of Congress with this billboard slogan: "Had Enough?" Truman understood this and demobilized the troops. He cut the number of civilian bureaucrats by half.

Truman saw the political reality in late 1946. Hazlitt saw his twin policies enacted by the end of 1946. This was his only victory in the book.

Further Reading

For support material, go to bit.ly/CEIOL-Doc-9.

–10–

The Fetish of
Full Employment

And Pharaoh commanded the same day the taskmas-
ters of the people, and their officers, saying, Ye shall no
more give the people straw to make brick, as heretofore:
let them go and gather straw for themselves. And the
tale of the bricks, which they did make heretofore, ye
shall lay upon them; ye shall not diminish ought there-
of: for they be idle; therefore they cry, saying, Let us go
and sacrifice to our God. Let there more work be laid
upon the men, that they may labour therein; and let
them not regard vain words (Exodus 5:6–9).

This passage should be familiar. I used it to begin Chapter 7: "The Curse of Machinery." I am using it again for a
simple reason: Chapter 10 is a recapitulation of Chapter 7. In
Chapter 10, Hazlitt presented a variation of the argument in
Chapter 7. In Chapter 7, he answered those critics of the free
market who rejected mechanization of the labor markets because this supposedly would displace workers. Here, he used
the same line of reasoning to refute critics of the free market
who insisted that the federal government must intervene into
the labor markets to guarantee full employment, which critics
insisted the free market could not do.

Pharaoh had three economic goals. First, he wanted full employment for Israelites—life without leisure. Second, he wanted the same output of bricks. Third, he wanted reduced costs:
the costs associated with producing straw, which Egyptian
taskmasters had previously borne. Straw was used in making

bricks. He turned the task of gathering straw over to the Israelites. In short, he wanted something for nothing: the same quantity of bricks, but cheaper for Egypt. But Pharaoh was a better economist than any Keynesian today. He knew there would not be something for nothing by means of a state decree. The Israelites would be forced to work harder.

There would be fuller employment: more work for the Israelites. Whatever free time they had possessed before Moses and Aaron challenged the authority of Pharaoh was now removed. Pharaoh punished them for the "vain words" that their covenantal representatives had spoken in his presence. He would show them who was in charge. The Israelites would bear the negative sanction of additional employment. The implication was clear: any further demands for a week's vacation to go and sacrifice to God would be followed by additional negative sanctions.

Pharaoh saw full employment as a negative sanction. So did the Israelites. In contrast, modern advocates of state intervention into the labor markets see full employment as a positive sanction. It is so positive, they argue, that voluntary contracts between employer and employees must be prohibited by law. The state must toss a stone.

A great benefit of the free market is this: it allows full employment for those who wish to work for a wage, and it allows leisure for those who do not. The only way that any society can gain both results is through an absence of state regulations over the labor markets. This is the "miracle of the market"—in the labor markets, as in all other markets. "But wait! There's more!" The free market also fosters full employment of all known resources, not just labor: land, raw materials, tools, and accurate information about economic conditions—past, present, and future.

1. Owners

There are multiple owners. The first owner is a person who owns capital. This capital includes a forecast regarding what customers will be willing and able to pay for a particular good or service in the future. He is an entrepreneur, for he possesses money, a forecast, and a plan to meet his forecast. The second owner is a worker who possesses the skills associated with producing this good or service. The third owner possesses scarce resources other than labor—resources that are crucial to the entrepreneur's plan of production. The fourth owner is the potential future customer who will own money at the time the good or service is brought to market.

Each possesses resources. Each has goals that may be attainable through a judicious application of their individual rights of ownership. In short, they possess opportunities for cooperation in the division of labor.

2. Window

These resource owners come together in a complex series of joint ventures. There is no central plan. The employer seeks employees at some wage, who in turn seek employment at some wage. If the wage is adjusted through competitive bidding, there will be no potential employees willing to work at that wage. There will also be no opportunities for the employer to increase his expected rate of profit by hiring an additional laborer. These are market-clearing wages, task by task. Then the employer will put them to work. He will also provide them with complementary factors of production: commercial land, tools, and raw materials. He puts up his own money, or money he has raised from investors and lenders, to make all this possible.

All of this is the product of a series of entirely voluntary contracts. These arrangements are not aspects of a central economic plan that was drawn up by any state official or agency. The owners of assets come together in the social division of labor. Each brings a unique resource to the production mix. Each seeks his own benefit.

There is full employment on this project. But this employment is not just the employment of labor. It is the employment of vision, money, capital, labor, tools, raw materials, and land.

All of this is a matter of competitive bidding. Employers compete against employers. Workers compete against workers. Resource owners compete against resource owners. Meanwhile, customers bide their time to see who will offer them the best deals when they finally decide to go shopping.

There is full employment . . . at specific prices. Why? *Because something is better than nothing.* Everyone wants a better deal, but there comes a time when any deal is better than no deal. The entire free market system is governed by, and motivated by, the most economically productive phrase in the history of man: "Let's make a deal." (This has been America's unofficial national slogan since about 1625.)

The window of the free market lets us see as through a glass, darkly. We all are looking for a better deal . . . at some price.

3. Stone

Incumbent politicians also want a deal. They want voters to re-elect them. So, they look for promises that will persuade voters to vote for them at the next election.

One appealing promise is this: the federal government can guarantee lots of jobs. The free market, they argue, has failed to provide full employment. But there is an asterisk: "at a living wage." This wage is a higher wage than employers are willing to pay. So, there are unemployed workers sitting around. There are also unemployed raw materials, tools, and commercial land. But few politicians look this closely at these other markets. They are interested in promoting full employment for workers, who vastly outnumber the owners of raw materials, tools, and commercial land.

The Great Depression in the 1930's was the result of prior central bank inflations in the 1920's, most notably in the United States, Great Britain, and Western Europe. When this boom turned into a bust after 1930, governments adopted Keynesian policies—half a decade before Keynes justified them in convoluted prose in *The General Theory* (1936). Herbert Hoover and the Republican Congress were pre-New Dealers in this regard. Governments in the West interfered with labor pricing, capital markets, and international trade. They all did this in the name of full employment. Nevertheless, unemployment remained high wherever forced labor was not imposed by socialist tyrants, who adopted either slave labor (USSR) or regimented labor (Nazi Germany).

Then, after nearly a decade of high unemployment, beginning on September 1, 1939, politicians in Europe found a politically effective way to overcome the unemployment of the Great Depression: World War II. This war led to regimented labor on a scale never before seen in the history of mankind. Governments drafted tens of millions of men into the armed forces. They encouraged tens of millions of women to replace these men in munitions factories. Then they taxed all adults who were not in the armed forces. The voters were willing to bear such taxes and regimentation in the name of military victory. It was "jobs for all." Everyone was paid a living wage until the bombs fell. Wages ceased for those directly under the bombs.

Central bankers inflated the various money supplies. This would have raised prices and wages, but all of the governments imposed price and wage controls—people controls—and political rationing. This reduced real wages, thereby increasing the demand for labor. (Remember economics' fundamental law: "At a lower price, more is demanded.") Presto: no more unemployment.

Then battlefield deaths reduced the work force. There were more jobs for the survivors. "Jobs for all!"

Then came the saturation bombings. This leveled cities. There was more work for rebuilding. "Jobs for all!"

World War II was the greatest government-imposed full employment program of the twentieth century. Wartime full employment is available to governments at any time. All that the voters need to do is recognize the reality of three unspoken words: "At some price." The price of World War II was

60 million deaths—a significant reduction of the work force, leading to higher employment rates.

When Hazlitt was writing his manuscript, it was widely feared that the pre-War rates of unemployment would reappear. The Full Employment Act of 1946 became law while he was writing his book.

He called full employment a fetish. It was a fetish for two reasons, First, there was the widespread fear of another depression: "no war, no full employment." Second, there was the fear of Keynesian economists and their disciples that without the central planning associated with war, which the public tolerated only for the sake of military victory, the labor markets would not clear through voluntary exchange. This is the universal fear of Keynesian economists. It defines them. Clausewitz wrote: "War is merely the continuation of policy by other means." *Keynesianism is merely the continuation of wartime central planning by other means.* Keynesians know that the public will not accept price controls and rationing in peacetime. But they promote the other wartime policies: government deficits and central bank monetization of debt.

Politicians, then as now, care about votes. Unemployed voters might vote incumbent politicians out of office. Politicians care deeply about productivity, but only of a special kind: generating votes. Full employment generates votes better than any other condition, economic or otherwise. Full employment is indeed a fetish—for voters and for politicians.

4. Costs

Political intervention into the economy results in a loss of liberty. This is always the highest cost. It is rarely mentioned. It is the most invisible of the things not seen.

People want to get richer from their labor. This requires tools—capital. It requires better information. It requires, in short, more investment per capita. People want to work more for part of their lives. But later they want to work less when their income per hour increases. They purchase leisure by forfeiting income from another hour of work. Leisure is a valuable consumer good, as the Israelites in Egypt understood. Pharaoh knew the secret of full employment: tyranny. Hazlitt understood this, too.

> Nothing is easier to achieve than full employment, once it is divorced from the goal of full production and taken as an end in itself. Hitler provided full employment with a huge armament program. The war provided full employment for every nation involved. The slave labor in Germany had full employment. Prisons and chain gangs have full employment. Coercion can always provide full employment.

This was the thing not seen in 1946. Yet it was right under the voters' noses. George Orwell was right: "To see what is in front of one's nose needs a constant struggle."

We do not want full employment. We want more productive employment: greater output per hour. We want easier employment. Again, quoting Hazlitt:

> The whole economic progress of mankind has consisted in getting more production with the same labor. It is for this reason that men began putting burdens on the backs of mules instead of on their own; that they went on to invent the wheel and the wagon, the railroad and the motor truck. It is for this reason that men used their ingenuity to develop 100,000 labor-saving inventions.

When we have no income, we want greater employment. But we do not want full employment: 16 hours a day. At some point, we want leisure. Some people want to be in the job market until they die. Others prefer retirement. In a free market, people can buy leisure by not having a job. They can also buy income by not having leisure.

Here is the rule: *You can't get something for nothing.* There are no free lunches. There are no free days off.

The central idea of a free society is liberty. Let people decide whether they want full employment, part-time employment, or no employment. Free markets make these choices available . . . at some price.

In the labor markets, state intervention reduces the number of offers of employment. Why? Because each intervention raises the costs of exchange. The fundamental economic law then goes into effect: "At a higher price, less is demanded."

Owners of resources find it more expensive to seek out owners of different assets who might be willing to make a deal. Even when they find such owners, the legislation has made it risky to arrange such an exchange. Therefore, black market exchanges become more frequent. Resources are shifted out of the legal, state-controlled markets into the illegal but un-controlled markets. The risk of detection rises. Costs rise in all markets. Fewer deals are demanded.

For employers who wish to stay out of black markets, there is a remedy: mechanization. Workers whose free market wag-es would have been sufficiently low to make uneconomic the introduction of labor-saving equipment are not allowed to of-fer their services at lower wages. So, employers buy machines. The job offers steadily disappear.

Government spending on mass employment projects must be paid for. Taxes rise. Government borrowing rises. Cen-tral bank monetary inflation rises. All of this reduces capital that would otherwise have gone into the private sector. Labor productivity is therefore reduced through a lack of capital. Workers must put up with poorer tools. It is the familiar sto-ry: shovels, not bulldozers. Shovel-ready government projects are not productive, except in terms of votes. But votes, not economic productivity, are the goal of politicians who vote for shovel-ready government projects.

5. Consequences

The inevitable result of such political policies is reduced production. Why? Higher costs, which reduce economic growth. The society is made poorer than it otherwise would have been.

Meanwhile, the federal bureaucracy increases in size and authority. Civil Service laws make it difficult to fire these employees.

Foreign workers whose nations do not imitate the Keynesian West are able to make arrangements with employers that are mutually beneficial. The productivity of these nations increases. Exports from these nations increase. Customers in the nations that are burdened by full employment laws find that they can find better deals in those sectors of the economy that are marked by imports. The impact of foreigners' productivity is felt in the nations that have adopted full-employment legislation. It is felt in the market for imported goods.

Exporters find that they benefit from indirect subsidies. The nation marked by full-employment laws suffers from reduced labor productivity and higher labor costs. This presents an opportunity to foreign exporters who do not suffer from such legislation. The result is full employment in the nations with no full employment laws on the books.

As Ludwig von Mises argued, the economic results of government intervention into the free markets are the opposite of the original justification of the intervention. But the results in the labor markets are consistent with the politicians' real goal, as distinguished from their official justification of the legislation. The real goal is more votes.

If more voters understood economics, the politicians would lose votes for passing such laws. But the voters do not understand economics. This is true of Christian voters. They do not understand economics, Christian or otherwise.

Conclusions

The Full Employment Act of 1946 was signed into law by President Truman on February 20, 1946. Hazlitt had just finished his manuscript. The low American unemployment rates of 1946–50 could be attributed to that law. But also in 1946, the elimination of wartime economic controls continued. Keynesians claim victory for low unemployment. So do free market economists.

There was a far better test case in West Germany. The Allied governments' wartime system of price controls, fiat money inflation (the Allies had special printing presses for occupation currency, which the Soviets demanded and were given), and rationing. Employment in legal markets was low. Black markets were everywhere.

Befginning in 1947, Ludwig Erhard became the director of the bi-zonal Office of Economic Opportunity. Dr. Erhard was a disciple of Wilhelm Röpke, who in turn was a disciple of Mises. On Sunday, June 20, 1948, Erhard went on the radio and announced a currency contraction of over 90%. Price controls were removed in the Western zone. The next day, the unemployment rate dropped sharply in the Western zone. People went back to work in the legal markets. That was the beginning of the so-called German economic miracle. It did not take place in the Soviet zone. It led to the most rapid economic development in history until 1978, when Deng Xiaoping announced a similar system of deregulation of China's agricultural sector.

The goal of full employment is legitimate. So is the goal of more leisure. So is the goal of service outside the wage system: non-profit volunteering. To achieve all three goals, men need liberty. They need to be able to make deals that they see as advantageous to them. They need the opportunity to make deals—lots and lots of deals. They can attain full employment, less employment, or no employment—as they see fit . . . at some price. They negotiate the price.

Further Reading

For supporting material, go to bit.ly/CEIOL-Doc-10.

–11–

Who's "Protected" by Tariffs?

And the LORD spake unto me, saying, Ye have compassed this mountain long enough: turn you northward. And command thou the people, saying, Ye are to pass through the coast of your brethren the children of Esau, which dwell in Seir; and they shall be afraid of you: take ye good heed unto yourselves therefore: Meddle not with them; for I will not give you of their land, no, not so much as a foot breadth; because I have given mount Seir unto Esau for a possession. Ye shall buy meat of them for money, that ye may eat; and ye shall also buy water of them for money, that ye may drink. (Deuteronomy 2:25)

God made it clear to Moses, who in turn made it clear to the Israelites, that there was to be free trade between the people of Israel and the people of Esau. There was to be no coercion. The people of Esau had goods that the Israelites wanted: meat and water. The people of Israel had what the people of Esau wanted: money. There were possibilities for voluntary exchange. The people of Israel were not in need of "protection" against the meat and water of Esau, meaning tariffs.

There is no mention of any tariff in the history of Israel in the Old Testament. There is none in the New Testament, either. The Roman Empire was a huge free trade zone. Its wealth rested on this fact. The Mediterranean had been cleared of pirates in 66 B.C. by Pompey. This increased trade. All roads led to Rome. This also increased trade.

1. Owners

In this incident, the owners were on both sides of the national border of Esau. There were the people of Esau, who possessed water and meat. There were the people of Israel, who possessed money. Because they had legal title to their property, they could pursue the best options available to them because of their property.

Because they owned their property, they possessed the legal right to disown it. Every piece of property was accompanied by a bundle of rights. This is the meaning of ownership: the right to use property in particular ways. One of these ways is exchange. The owners of these rights sought ways to increase their possession of more desirable goods through exchange. Who decided which goods were more desirable? Their owners.

Today, there are owners who are affected by tariffs. Buyers (customers) on both sides of a national border are owners of money. Sellers (producers) on both sides are owners of goods. They are beneficiaries of a moral and legal order that allows them to do what they want with whatever they own, including the surrender of ownership.

There are also producers of goods on both sides of the border who face competition from sellers on the other side. They own resources. They seek to maximize their income from these resources. They have an incentive to restrict competition.

2. Window

The window was the legal system governing each of these nations. In the area of exchange, each civil order allowed the exchange of goods across the national border. Neither system of laws imposed restrictions on exchange. This is what free trade means.

"Free trade" usually has a more narrow focus than "free market." But they are the same. The free market is a product of a legal system that allows free trade: across the street, across the county line, across the state line, and across the national line. The institutional arrangement places owners as judicially sovereign over whatever they own. The invisible judicial lines known as borders have no economic impact on the legal rights of people on opposite sides of these borders to exchange goods.

The bundle of rights associated with the ownership of specific pieces of property is conveyed across all borders: street, county, state, and national. There are no discriminatory taxes placed on the person who is selling one form of property across a border: goods. There is equality under the law. This conforms to the most fundamental civil law of Moses: equality before the law. "One law shall be to him that is homeborn, and unto the stranger that sojourneth among you" (Exodus 12:49).

On both sides of the border, free men possess the legal right to make bids to sell goods (producers), as well as the legal right to buy goods (customers). This legal order enables them to exercise the rights of ownership. Because they possess the right to trade, they can specialize in whatever activities they do best in the marketplace—"best" being determined by paying customers.

3. Stone

Tariffs are sales taxes on imported goods. These sales taxes are collected by the national civil government. They are, in the language of the criminal syndicates, protection money. But instead of protecting customers from imported goods, tariffs are imposed on importers. This reduces demand for imported goods, according to this fundamental economic: "When prices rise, less is demanded." So, the "protection money" is collected from importers. Then who is being protected? Domestic producers of the taxed items. They can more readily undercut the prices of the imported goods, plus tariffs.

The politicians of the national state come before the voters and propose sales taxes on goods that cross into the nation from abroad. The politicians are careful not to describe these sales taxes as sales taxes. Too many voters are tired of paying the existing level of taxes, let alone a new tax. So, the politicians call these sales taxes by a new name: tariffs.

Politicians not only play word games. They play logical games. They tell the voters that these sales taxes—never called sales taxes—will make the nation richer. Voters who would normally hoot in derision line up to support these sales taxes. After all, these taxes will make the nation richer. How? By protecting the domestic population against unscrupulous cut-throat foreigners. The phrase "cut-throat" is a code phrase for "discount."

Voters who are always in search of discounts recoil in horror at the accusation of "cut-throat competition." Politicians then add the adjective "unfair." The voters demand that the politicians take action to protect them. They demand the imposition of tariffs. Tariffs will make them all richer, they conclude. It is as if a nation of vegetarians demanded that politicians legalize cannibalism, but only after politicians re-name cannibalism as "dietary protein supplements."

4. Costs

The initial loss comes from having to pay a sales tax on an item that would have been be tax-free, had it been produced on this side of the border. The state gets richer at the expense of the import buyers. This pleases employees of the state, who are in a position to spend more money in their family budgets. The budgets of state bureaucrats is thereby protected from the unconscionable spending of those members of the public who bought items from abroad.

Yet this was not the argument of the politicians who persuaded the voters to accept a program of domestic protection. The voters were not thinking about protecting the incomes of bureaucrats. That is the first thing not seen by the voters.

Next, there are the losses sustained by the voters who were ready to purchase an imported good, but who did not do so after the sales tax increased the sales price. Their range of choice is diminished by higher prices. This is the second thing not seen by the voters.

Next, there are those voters who bought instead from a domestic supplier. But the domestic supplier was able to ask and receive a price higher than the price that would have prevailed, had the imported good been available without the sales tax. The difference in prices was transferred to the domestic producer out of the budgets of the buyers. This is the third thing not seen by the voters.

Next, there are the suppliers of goods and services to those voters who would have spent the money they would have saved, had they been able to buy at a lower price as a result of the lower prices. They will not make the sales. Their prospective customers are now poorer. This is the fourth thing not seen by the voters.

Next, there are the sellers on the other side of the border who did not sell to the importer. Of course the voters don't care about him, the foul cut-throat. But that ruthless cut-throat now has no domestic currency available from buyers on the domestic side of the border. Since he had no way to spend that money on his side of the border—it all looks like play money to people on his side of the border—he had intended to buy things on the domestic side of the border. So, those exporters on the domestic side of the border will not make a sale abroad. This is the fifth thing not seen by voters.

Then there are all the businesses that would have sold goods to the exporters. No sales for them. This is the sixth thing not seen by the voters.

Let's say that a majority of politicians come up with this sports strategy for the nation. From this point on, all foreigners choosing to compete against the nation's athletes inside the nation's borders will be forced to wear ankle braces weighing anywhere from two pounds to five pounds, depending on the skills of the domestic contenders. Will the nation's athletes win more medals at these domestic events? No doubt about it. This will increase their self-esteem, say the politicians. "We do not want to send our young people into world competition when they have no self esteem."

But, you say, this strategy will lead to fewer gold medals at the Olympics. Our athletes will not be able to compete with world-class athletes. Clearly, you do not understand the idea of fair competition in domestic sports. Those foreign athletes are nothing less than cut-throat competitors. The public prefers slower race times and lower high jumping, but more victories by nationals. It is better to forget about the Olympics. It is best to boycott the Olympics. Who needs them?

Now apply this logic to foreign economic competition.

Let us return to domestic economic competition. Because imports are restricted, domestic industries do not have to face competition from abroad. Domestic manufacturers do not keep up with the latest innovations. There is no need to.

Meanwhile, because sales taxes on imports lead to reduced exports, the export sector of the domestic economy does not grow as rapidly as it would otherwise have grown. Domestic industries are increasingly isolated from the international markets. This hands over international markets to foreign producers. This is the seventh thing not seen by the voters.

At last, we come to the winners: successful sellers of high-priced goods on this side of the border. They, their employees, and their suppliers are flush with cash. They have been protected, as promised by the politicians. But they have not been protected at zero price to the majority of the domestic population. The public has paid its protection money to the state and the minority of the special-interest groups favored by the state. These winners are visible. There are always visible winners when the state tosses a stone through a window.

We now have an answer to the chapter's title, "Who's protected by tariffs?" It is not the vast majority of voters who are protected. It is a fallacy to imagine that benefits are available, net, to the population as a result of sales taxes on imports. Haziltt was correct.

> But the fallacy comes from looking merely at this manufacturer and his employees, or merely at the Ameri-

can sweater industry. It comes from noticing only the results that are immediately seen, and neglecting the results that are not seen because they are prevented from coming into existence.

5. Consequences

Tariff politics is the politics of special interests. It is the politics of back-room deals. It is the politics of political action committees and donations to the committee to re-elect Jones.

Inherently, the vast majority of voters are uninterested in specific pieces of legislation. This is where the 1,000-page bills that no politician reads turn into 2,000-page bills that no politician reads. The voters do not follow the economic logic of all of the special-interest legislation that winds up in these bills. But the special interests are intensely interested. There is a great deal of money on the line.

Tariffs are never discussed as sales taxes. More of the voters would be alerted to the economics of tariffs if tariffs were properly labeled. There are no government laws mandating truth in labeling when it comes to Congress.

Nevertheless, there have been consistent reductions in tariffs since 1947, and especially after 1960. The General Agreement of Tariffs and Trade was set up in 1947. The percentage of the GDP of the United States generated by imports and exports has risen to about a quarter. In 1946, it was around six percent. The GATT was an international organization. It promoted managed trade, as does its successor, the World Trade Organization. But tariffs were reduced, and trade did increase.

Most economists favor free trade. Here is one area of the economy in which proponents of high tariffs cannot get support from academic economists. Also, multinational American-based corporations make far larger contributions to political action committees than small special interest groups do.

Conclusions

Hazlitt's concerns in 1946 had to do with tariffs, not managed trade, which had not yet come into existence. He was responding to widely held public opinion. But, in this instance, widely held public opinion has had a declining influence in governments. Large-scale special interest groups that favor increased international trade have been dominant.

Hazlitt identified the economic issue: the broken window fallacy.

> Thus all the chief tariff fallacies stem from the central fallacy with which this book is concerned. They are the result of looking only at the immediate effects of a single tariff rate on one group of producers, and forgetting the long-run effects both on consumers as a whole and on all other producers.

Here is a case where the national government has decided to reduce the number of stones. I do not think Hazlitt persuaded them. This was crucial. The dominance of the U.S. economy after World War II was so great that the export sector boomed. Post-War Europe and Japan could not compete. American firms invested abroad. They became multinational. Then they shipped goods back into the United States. This raised imports, as rising exports always do. The special economic interests that were dominant politically in 1970, when international competition from Japan and Western Europe finally became competitive in the United States, favored low tariffs. So did GATT. Congress went along. One result was the destruction of the trade union movement in the private sector. Manufacturing employment declined as a percentage of the American economy. So did union membership after 1953.

The voters, paying little attention, did not fight this.

Further Reading

For supporting material, go to bit.ly/CEIOL-Doc-11.

–12–

The Drive for Exports

And the LORD spake unto me, saying, Ye have compassed this mountain long enough: turn you northward. And command thou the people, saying, Ye are to pass through the coast of your brethren the children of Esau, which dwell in Seir; and they shall be afraid of you: take ye good heed unto yourselves therefore: Meddle not with them; for I will not give you of their land, no, not so much as a foot breadth; because I have given mount Seir unto Esau for a possession. Ye shall buy meat of them for money, that ye may eat; and ye shall also buy water of them for money, that ye may drink. (Deuteronomy 2:25)

This should be familiar. You read it in Chapter 11: "Who's 'Protected' by Tariffs?" Why do I reprint it here? Because this chapter raises the same issue: the nation-state's violation of free trade. Chapter 11 dealt with legal limits on goods coming in: sales taxes. This chapter deals with tax subsidies on goods going out. In both cases, the laws subsidize special interest groups at the expense of customers.

God made it clear to Moses, who in turn made it clear to the Israelites, that there was to be free trade between the people of Israel and the people of Esau. There was to be no coercion. The people of Esau had goods that the Israelites wanted: meat and water. The people of Israel had what the people of Esau wanted: money. There were possibilities for voluntary exchange. The people of Israel were not in need of "protection" against the meat and water of Esau, meaning tariffs.

There is no mention of any export subsidy in the history of Israel in the Old Testament. There is none in the New Testament, either. The Roman Empire was a huge free trade zone. Its wealth rested on this fact. The Mediterranean had been cleared of pirates in 66 B.C. by Pompey. This increased trade. All roads led to Rome. This also increased trade.

1. Owners

In this incident, the owners were on both sides of the national border of Esau. There were the people of Esau, who possessed water and meat. There were the people of Israel, who possessed money. Because they had legal title to their property, they could pursue the best options available to them because of their property.

Because they owned their property, they possessed the legal right to disown it. Every piece of property was accompanied by a bundle of rights. This is the meaning of ownership: the right to use property in particular ways. One of these ways is exchange. The owners of these rights sought ways to increase their possession of more desirable goods through exchange. Who decided which goods were more desirable? Their owners.

Today, there are owners who are affected by export subsidies. Buyers (customers) on both sides of a national border are owners of money. Sellers (producers) on both sides are owners of goods. They are beneficiaries of a moral and legal order that allows them to do what they want with whatever they own, including the surrender of ownership.

There are also producers of goods on both sides of the border who face competition from sellers on the other side. They own resources. They seek to maximize their income from these resources. They have an incentive to get a government subsidy.

2. Window

The window was the legal system governing each of these nations. In the area of exchange, each civil order allowed the exchange of goods across the national border. Neither system of laws authorized tax subsidies for exchange. This is what free trade means.

"Free trade" usually has a more narrow focus than "free market." But they are the same. The free market is a product of a legal system that allows free trade: across the street, across the county line, across the state line, and across the national line. The institutional arrangement places owners as judicially sovereign over whatever they own. The invisible judicial lines known as borders have no economic impact on the legal rights of people on opposite sides of these borders to exchange goods.

The bundle of rights associated with the ownership of specific pieces of property is conveyed across all borders: street, county, state, and national. There are no tax-funded subsidies provided to the person who is selling one form of property across a border: goods. There is equality under the law. This conforms to the most fundamental civil law of Moses: equality before the law. "One law shall be to him that is homeborn, and unto the stranger that sojourneth among you" (Exodus 12:49).

On both sides of the border, free men possess the legal right to make bids to sell goods (producers), as well as the legal right to buy goods (customers). This legal order enables them to exercise the rights of ownership. Because they possess the right to trade, they can specialize in whatever activities they do best in the marketplace—"best" being determined by paying customers.

3. Stone

The politicians want votes. They seek votes from special-interest groups that are politically organized to persuade politicians to provide government subsidies. This reduces their costs of operation.

Producers in export-based industries face competition from producers that sell to residents. Firms in both sectors bid up the cost of the production goods they require. This reduces profit margins. The exporters want to gain an advantage over producers who cater to domestic residents. So, they take advantage of the still-popular economics of seventeenth-century mercantilism. They call for government subsidies, either direct or indirect. A direct subsidy would be a below-market rate on a business loan provided by the government. An indirect subsidy would be a government guarantee of full reimbursement if foreigners refuse to buy the exported products. The loan now has virtually no risk. The government has put its credit rating on the line on behalf of the exporting firm. This is co-signing (Chapter 6). The exporter can take this written guarantee to its banks and ask for a lower interest rate. This subsidizes a shift of capital away from the market for domestic goods into the market for exported goods.

4. Costs

Who puts up the money for a direct loan to an exporting firm? The government. Who pays the government? Taxpayers. Who pays the money-losing exporter if an exported good does not make a profit? The government. Who pays the government? Taxpayers.

But there is more to it than the money involved. There are also the losses imposed on domestic customers. When a foreigner buys a subsidized good, that good leaves the nation. Residents now have fewer goods to choose from. There was foreign money that came to the exporting firm. The firm can buy the domestic currency with this foreign currency. It can then reward its employees. It can continue to buy from its domestic suppliers of capital goods. But this means that the various domestic producers that would have gotten sales do not get sales. This is the broken window effect. Nobody notices what did not happen. They notice only those things that did happen.

Domestic customers go into the retail markets in search of bargains. Where are the bargains? Nowhere. Why not? Because the goods that were exported are not available for purchase by residents of the nation. Also, some of the residents are poorer as a result of the taxes paid to the government to supply the export subsidy money.

Meanwhile, on the other side of the border, some customers are better off. Had there not been a subsidy to exporters on the other side of the border, these foreign consumers would have done without. They love export subsidies on the other side of the border. But, of course, foreign producers who could have gained domestic sales miss out. The subsidies on imported goods made the foreign-produced goods too attractive. It was not that these domestic producers were not efficient. They just did not receive a subsidy from across the border.

5. Consequences

The availability of exported categories of goods is reduced. This keeps prices higher than they would otherwise have been in these markets. The customers do not understand why. That is because of the broken window factor.

Because prices are higher for categories of goods that have been sent abroad, domestic customers are worse off. They are poorer than they otherwise would have been. They will have to restrict their consumption through no economic fault of their own. (If they voted for politicians who voted for export subsidies, then these citizens are at fault politically. They are at fault for not understanding economics.)

On the other side of the border, there is now political agitation by those domestic manufacturers who are facing subsidized goods from across the border. They will call on their politicians to do something to offset this unfair competition from across the border. (They have a point. This subsidized competition really is unfair . . . to the taxpayers and customers across the border.) They will push for tariffs and quotas. A trade war could begin. This sequence of events happened during the Great Depression of the 1930's, making it last longer.

If the country whose politicians voted for the export subsidies also imposes tariffs and quotas, then the two policies are schizophrenic. The export subsidies increase the amount of foreign currency owned by the exporting companies. What can these companies do with this foreign money in foreign banks? How about this? They can use this money to invest in foreign businesses that export goods. Oops! The tariffs and quotas in the nation that subsidize exports inevitably reduce the amount of imports. So, politicians who vote for tariffs and also for export subsidies are like politicians who vote for agricultural subsidies to domestic tobacco farmers, and then vote for anti-smoking laws.

Conclusions

The phrase "free market" means free trade. The legal order that establishes private property by definition establishes free trade. The right to *own* property necessarily implies the right to *disown* property. Free trade is based on freedom to exchange ownership across borders: streets, counties, states, and nations.

We find that people who assure us that they believe in private property in fact do not. They believe in state-regulated trade, meaning the prohibition of disownership. When someone says, "You can't buy that," this means "you can't sell this." If I cannot legally buy goods from across a national border, then I cannot legally transfer my money to someone on the other side of that border, except as a gift.

Export subsidies are not gifts to foreigners. They are foreign aid programs. They are disguised foreign aid. It is government money handed over to exporters. This leads to the transfer of goods out of the nation to foreign customers.

But it works both ways. Foreign aid programs are disguised export subsidies. The government gives taxpayers' money to foreign governments. These foreign governments use this money—the domestic currency of the aid-giving nation—to buy goods from exporters in the aid-giving nation. This supports exports. It necessarily reduces the quantity of goods in the aid-giving nation. The taxpayers lose, and domestic customers lose.

It makes no difference what politicians call it: "foreign aid" or "export subsidies." The economic results are similar. **Wealth is transferred abroad by the politicians**. Different companies benefit: foreign aid vs. export subsidies. But the net result is reduced national wealth.

There are voters who say, "The federal government should stop giving foreign aid." Then they support export subsidies. They are intellectually confused.

What is the correct view, biblically speaking? Free trade and free markets, which are the same thing. Let individual Israelites and individual Edomites make deals if they want to. The governments on both sides of the border should stay out of the markets: no sales taxes on imports and no subsidies for exports.

Further Reading

For supporting material, go to bit.ly/CEIOL-Doc-12.

"Parity" Prices

It is naught, it is naught, saith the buyer: but when he is gone his way, then he boasteth (Proverbs 20:14).

Every voluntary exchange involves buying and selling. The person who is called a buyer is a seller of money. He buys goods and services. The person who is called a seller is a buyer of money. He sells something of value to purchase money.

The practice described here by Solomon is familiar. In negotiating, both the buyer of goods and the buyer of money complain that the asking price is too high. It is not a good enough deal. "It is naught, it is naught." Each hopes that the seller will drop his price. In the case of the buyer of money (seller of goods), he hopes that the buyer of goods (seller of money) will decide to take less for his money. Solomon knew that his listeners and readers would recognize this negotiating technique.

The technique rests on this institutional arrangement: the right to bid. We can see this in markets in which private property is secure (the window). We also see it in markets governed by politics (the stone).

In a society with a small retail market, where there are few rival options nearby, negotiation is basic to sales. In a highly developed economy, there is not much negotiation. We do not negotiate with a check-out clerk when we get to the front of the line at a supermarket. The clerk scans the bar code on the item's package, and the computer adds it to the list of items we are buying. The negotiation rule here is clear: "Take it or leave it." It is easy to leave it. Anyone can shop at a different store, or go online to check prices.

Sellers (buyers of money) bid against sellers. Buyers (sellers of money) bid against buyers. Out of this competitive bidding process—a gigantic auction system—come objective prices. There is little ignorance. Face-to-face negotiating is limited to zones of ignorance regarding prices and quality. *The better the information about market prices, the narrower the range for price negotiating.*

1. Owners

There are several groups of owners, as always.

One group owns money, which is the most marketable commodity. Economists classify these people under the classification of consumers. They are sellers of money and buyers of goods to consume. In this case, the goods are food.

Another group is made up of owners of natural resources—in this case, commodities. Economists classify natural resources under the general category of land. In this case, the land owners are farmers.

There are other owners. They own commodities, but only temporarily. They are intermediaries in between land owners and final consumers. They are producers. They purchase raw materials, labor services, and buy or rent capital in order to transform raw materials into final products. Producers are not final consumers. They are buyers, but they are also sellers. They buy in order to make a profit: buy low, sell high. They can be classified under the category of customers. In this case, they are part of the food production and distribution system. The obvious example would be a baker.

There is a fourth group: retailers. They buy goods that contain restructured commodities. They sell these to consumers. They own these commodities temporarily. A supermarket where food is sold is an example.

There is a fifth group: owners of forecasts regarding the future. They may be able to sell this information. They may choose to give it away. Until this subjective information affects actual bids in the marketplace, it is irrelevant to the pricing system. But whenever these people put their money where their forecasts are, by buying or selling commodity futures contracts, they become speculators. Their bids affect prices at the margin: up or down.

There is a biblical case of rival forecasts of the supply and demand for food. The capital city of Samaria was under siege. Food prices had skyrocketed. At this point, Elisha the prophet came before the king and predicted that the next day, food prices would be low. He was ridiculed by an officer. Elisha told the guard that he would not taste of this food. That night, the siege ended. The army fled. They left food behind. The next day, people in the city streamed out of the city to get free food. They trampled the king's officer (II Kings 6-7). In the terminology of the commodity futures market, Elisha was a "short." He expected prices to fall. The officer was a "long." He expected prices to stay high. In this case, the guard lost a lot more than money.

Because owners have the right to own, they also have the right to disown whatever they own. They can legally sell. They can legally make an exchange. This brings us to the window.

2. Window

Consumers compete against consumers. Producers compete against producers. Raw materials owners compete against raw materials owners. Owners of capital compete against owners of capital. Commodity futures speculators compete against each other: "longs" vs. "shorts." **Out of this bidding process comes an array of prices**. The economic order in a free market system is based on a series of auctions. The same rule of exchange governs all of them: "High bid wins."

The average person knows what an auction is. He understands why the high bid wins. He understands that bidders compete against bidders. But a free market economist has a major educational task: to persuade the general public that the orderliness and fairness of an auction is a legitimate model for

the entire economy. The principle of open bidding will produce an equally orderly and equally fair economy. The ability
to make this application of logic—from a local auction to an
international auction—is a limited resource. This is demonstrated by over two centuries of resistance to the the idea of
free trade, which is most famously argued in Adam Smith's
Wealth of Nations (1776).

The average person can easily understand and readily approve of the allocation principle of "high bid wins" at an auction. One of the tasks I have set for myself in writing this book
is to help readers make the conceptual transition from "high
bid wins" at a local auction to "high bid wins" for every transaction. This is more easily said than done.

In the auction markets (plural) for commodities, the principle
of "high bid wins" benefits those buyers and sellers who come to
an agreement on a price. There are multiple sub-markets in this
and every other market. The initial market is established between commodity owners and producers. The second phase of
the market is established between producers and middlemen:
retailers. The final stage is the transaction between retailers and
consumers. At every step, the rule is "high bid wins."

This principle of distribution annoys those who do not make
the highest bid. Sometimes this annoys them so much that
they form a political action group that campaigns for legislation that restricts the use of "high bid wins." People who ran
out of money before the auction was over demand that the
state impose legal price ceilings. But high bids come on both
sides of a transaction. Sometimes those sellers of commodities who were forced to take too low a price, and who dropped
out of the auction in order to avoid a loss, see an opportunity.
They may be able to persuade the government to make lower
bids illegal. This leads us to this chapter's stone.

3. Stone

Here is a major problem for economists who believe in the
free market. There are few of them. They have to overcome

the logic of other economists who believe in the free market for some resources, but not all. I have read a lot of economics books. I have yet to see any economics book with this title: *The Free Market as an Auction*. I think most economists see the market process in this way, but they rarely argue for this understanding of the market process. I do not know why this is the case, but I have my suspicions. I think they worry about this: the idea that the government should place a lid on prices at an auction is clearly ridiculous. It would destroy the auction. No auctioneers would show up. Neither would bidders. No one wants to attend a rigged auction. But if price ceilings destroy an auction, and if the free market is an auction, then there is no economic case for price ceilings. Therefore, any economist who wants to argue in favor of a price ceiling at any time prefers to avoid discussing the free market as an auction. The logic of his presentation would undermine him every time he calls for a price ceiling. No one wants to appear inconsistent. So, economists refrain from describing the free market as an auction.

Even less logical is the economist who would argue this way: "It would be beneficial to buyers if there were government controls that force the opening bid to be higher than anyone is willing to pay." This policy also would kill the auction. People come to an auction expecting a bidding to begin by an initial bid. If the government were to come in and forbid low bids, and then buy the goods at a high price, prospective buyers would stop showing up. They would know that they will be outbid by the government, which can afford to outbid them. The auction is rigged.

Now let us consider agriculture. The farmers own land. They own knowledge. They own money, which they use to buy the tools of production. They own credit: their reputations for repayment of debt. They sell their crops to wholesalers, who in turn sell to manufacturers, who in turn sell to consumers. Consumers possess money. They determine, retroactively, which of the producers in this chain of service served them best. Their decisions to buy from some and not buy from others make some farmers rich and others poor.

The farmers act as economic agents of the final consumers. All of the producers do.

In the days of Solomon, every buyer and every seller had an opportunity to announce: "It is naught, it is naught." Haggling slowed down the speed of decision-making. In the modern economy, there is almost no haggling. This is because of the nature of the window: the free market's auction system reduces ignorance regarding supply and demand.

The agricultural markets have long been the most developed of markets. This is especially true of the grains. Grains are easily judged in terms of quality and type. There are professionals who make these assessments.

The free market in agricultural products is international. It is gigantic. There are hundreds of millions of farmers and billions of consumers of food. Most of these farms are small. They are in villages in China and India. They sell little food outside their villages. About three million farms feed most of the world's urban populations. In the United States, about 200,000 farms produce 80% of the agricultural output. These farmers have access to the World Wide Web. This means that price information is widespread. The food markets are international. Prices are established by competitive bidding to a fraction of any currency unit.

There is another important aspect of the grain markets: commodity futures trading. Speculators can enter these markets with a low payment of earnest money and make bids. Some of them bid to buy a large quantity of grain in the future at some price. They "go long." Others bid to deliver a large quantity of grain in the future at some price. They "go short." These speculators make a lot of money if they guess correctly about the future price of the particular grain. This opportunity for highly leveraged profits lures sophisticated forecasters into this market. The losses cull out the losers. The survivors are very good guessers.

This system of competitive bidding establishes preliminary prices for each of the grains. This price information is public. It is made available on the Web to farmers and wholesale grain buyers at no cost to them. Grain prices change, minute by minute. This means that there is a very narrow range for price negotiating. The ignorance factor is minimal. No one bothers to cry out, "It is naught, it is naught." The answer is clear: "If you can buy it cheaper somewhere, you can make a fortune with arbitrage. Buy low in one market and sell high simultaneously in another." In short, "Put your money where your mouth is." This silences most people.

Under this system of decentralized international farming, efficient farmers are rewarded. Inefficient farmers leave the field (literally). In 1800, at least 90% of the American population lived on farms. Today, this is down to 2%. American grain agriculture is the most efficient on earth. It has been since the 1840's: the reaper, the railroads, and the grasslands. About 30% of American farm income comes from exports.

With this as background, let us consider parity agricultural prices in the United States. The Agricultural Adjustment Act of 1933 established a federal loan program for farmers. Farmers could borrow money at below-market rates. They could then plant crops. In 1938, the Act was modified. Farmers who took these loans were guaranteed parity prices—above-market prices, as it turned out. They were paid these prices for up to 75% of their output. This loan/parity price program still is in force. This reduces the participating farmers' risk of economic failure in the next planting season.

To make these government-guaranteed prices predictable, a complex formula is applied. A particular year is selected as the base year. Then the highest price paid for that crop in the base year is established as the government purchase price in the next year. If the market price falls below this price—called a parity price—the government buys the crop and stores it.

The special-interest farming group tries to persuade the politicians to select a base year in which there was a high price for that crop. Why not a year in which the crop sold for less? The special-interest group has an answer: "It is naught, it is naught."

Instead of letting the international markets establish the price of a crop, moment by moment, in terms of supply and demand, American politicians have intervened. A majority of them vote every year to guarantee a minimum price for most of the crops of farms that enroll in the program. If, in international markets, prices are lower than a guaranteed price, those farms that participate in the subsidy program will sell their crop to the government. They will receive an indirect subsidy from taxpayers.

One official justification for parity prices is this: these prices will guarantee that family farms will not go out of business. What has been the result? In 1930, about 25% of the U.S. population lived on farms. Today, it is 2%.

Another justification: these guaranteed prices will assure a steady, reliable source of food. The people who use this argument assume that the voters will not pay any attention to international grain markets, which are gigantic, and which have supplied a steady supply of food for over two hundred years. Except for the Irish potato famine in the 1840's, the West has never suffered a famine during peacetime.

With parity pricing, the farmers become the economic agents of the government rather than the consumers. They profit or lose in terms of prices arbitrarily established by bureaucrats, not consumers. The locus of authority shifts from fickle customers to tenured bureaucrats. Tenured bureaucrats are far easier to predict than consumers. Above the bureaucrats (at least in theory), politicians are far easier to persuade than consumers. The farm bloc has an easier time of things dealing with politicians than consumers.

4. Costs

First, consumers of food in the parity-price nation have a competitor in the food markets: the national government.

The government can afford to buy up a large percentage of the crops in years in which prices on world markets are lower than the parity price. The crops bought by the government would have been brought to the marketplace. Sellers of crops would have competed against each other to sell all of their crops. Food prices would have been lower. But these crops are bought by the government and put into storage. This limits the supply of storage facilities, thereby raising costs.

Second, taxpayers must pay money to the government, so that the government can buy the nation's crops, or a large percentage of them, depending on the political pricing process.

In most cases, these two groups are the same. So, taxpayers are taxed so that they will have to pay higher prices for their food. They will have less money to spend, and they will have to spend more money on food.

The general public is generally unaware of all this. Otherwise, they might elect politicians who would vote against the farm-bloc politicians who vote for parity prices for agricultural products. The cry of the consumer-taxpayers would be this: "It is naught, it is naught." But they remain unaware.

Chapter 6 is "Credit Diverts Production." Parity prices and below-market interest rates on agricultural loans lure farmers into producing crops in an economy that would otherwise produce other goods and services. Consumers of food also want other things to consume. But their bids for other goods and services are reduced, first by taxes to pay for the farm bloc's surplus crops that are stored by the government or given away as foreign aid, and second by higher food prices at the supermarket. The consumers' range of choices is thereby reduced. This is another way of saying consumers are poorer than they otherwise would have been.

5. Consequences

In the United States, where this system has prevailed ever since 1933, there has been a steady reduction in the number of family farms. Today, the percentage of the American population that is directly involved in farming is somewhere in the range of 2%. To this could be added another 13% of the population that works in industries related to agriculture.

According to recent statistics, about 97% of these farms and ranches are family-owned. But large farms that sell at least $250,000 of crops annually account for over 80% of all sales. These farms constitute about 10% of all farms. Consider what we would expect the distribution to be. The famous 20-80 Pareto curve would have estimated that 20% of the farms would produce 80% of the output. Normally, about 20% of the members of any group or industry provide about 80% of the output. This has been known ever since it was discovered by the Italian economist Vilfredo Pareto in 1897.

Why is the American agricultural production system skewed toward inequality far more narrow at the top than the Pareto curve would have predicted? The first place to look for an answer is government intervention into the farming industry. The parity system has done nothing to enable small farms to compete with large farms. If anything, the system has offered greater subsidies to large farms. The parity program is a program that subsidizes rich farmers at the expense of middle class food buyers. This has been true from the beginning.

Conclusion

The multibillion-dollar agribusiness industry, dominated in the United States by four companies, has used the image of the family farm to extract wealth from taxpayers and food eaters. The voters pay no attention. This is a classic example of how special-interest legislation is signed into law. Voters are not focused on how much any piece of special-interest legislation is costing them. They do not organize politically to defeat such legislation. In contrast, the richest members of a tiny economic sector—2% of the U.S. population—are intensely focused on getting their legislative agenda through the political system.

There is political asymmetry here: information and motivation. The costs of organizing a decentralized voter base are very high. The risk of failure to organize them into a resistance voting bloc is also high. In contrast, the costs of organizing a tiny special-interest producers' group are low, and the benefits from a successful political campaign are high.

I would like to think that you will remember this every time you eat anything. But you won't. It would spoil your appetite. But if you say grace at meals, think of this: God's grace has been so great that it has overcome the federal government's parity price boondoggle for four gigantic multibillion-dollar agribusiness firms. You paid more for the meal than you would have paid without this boondoggle, but God in His grace, by means of an overwhelmingly free market in agricultural products, has put food on your table. Once in a while, you should pray for more grace and lower parity prices.

Further Reading

For supporting material, go to bit.ly/CEIOL-Doc-13.

-14-

Saving the X Industry

And the same time there arose no small stir about that way. For a certain man named Demetrius, a silversmith, which made silver shrines for Diana, brought no small gain unto the craftsmen; Whom he called together with the workmen of like occupation, and said, Sirs, ye know that by this craft we have our wealth. Moreover ye see and hear, that not alone at Ephesus, but almost throughout all Asia, this Paul hath persuaded and turned away much people, saying that they be no gods, which are made with hands: So that not only this our craft is in danger to be set at nought; but also that the temple of the great goddess Diana should be despised, and her magnificence should be destroyed, whom all Asia and the world worshippeth. And when they heard these sayings, they were full of wrath, and cried out, saying, Great is Diana of the Ephesians (Acts 19:23–28).

The Apostle Paul unquestionably preached that idols are not gods. Unquestionably, the silversmiths at Ephesus were at risk of suffering reduced demand for their output. The message that Paul brought challenged people's faith in the power of the idols produced by Ephesian silversmiths. This loss of faith would have reduced demand for all idols. The silversmiths at Ephesus responded by fomenting a riot.

The local Roman bureaucrat spoke to the crowd. He did not invoke the familiar cry of the potential loss of employment as a result of reduced consumer demand. Instead, he called on the crowd to calm down.

> And when the townclerk had appeased the people, he said, Ye men of Ephesus, what man is there that knoweth not how that the city of the Ephesians is a worshipper of the great goddess Diana, and of the image which fell down from Jupiter? Seeing then that these things cannot be spoken against, ye ought to be quiet, and to do nothing rashly. For ye have brought hither these men, which are neither robbers of churches, nor yet blasphemers of your goddess. Wherefore if Demetrius, and the craftsmen which are with him, have a matter against any man, the law is open, and there are deputies: let them implead one another. But if ye inquire any thing concerning other matters, it shall be determined in a lawful assembly. For we are in danger to be called in question for this day's uproar, there being no cause whereby we may give an account of this concourse. And when he had thus spoken, he dismissed the assembly (vv. 35–41).

He instructed them to bring any charges against Paul to the court. He invoked the rule of law. He had in mind Roman law, but the same principle of law had long been the standard in Mosaic Israel: "One law shall be to him that is homeborn, and unto the stranger that sojourneth among you" (Exodus 12:49).

The judicial principle of the rule of law means that the civil government must not create special-interest legislation that favors one industry over another. If an industry begins to suffer a decline in demand because of changing beliefs or changing tastes among the masses of buyers, the state is not to intervene to defend it. The official did not call on Paul to cease preaching, nor did he offer a direct subsidy to silversmiths involved in manufacturing idols.

It would be better for customers and taxpayers today if the modern state adopted the same hands-off principle.

1. Owners

There were owners of silver who had developed a steady income by selling idols. They owned tools used in their trade. They also possessed certain skills related to their craft, which included knowledge of the markets for idols. There were also secondary owners: people who owned silver, people who rented space to the tradesmen, and people associated with transport.

Then there were people who owned money. They were potential buyers of idols of Diana. They possessed the most marketable commodity: money.

2. Window

There was a market for these idols. This means that there were frequent sales. It was a predictable market, within limits. But Paul's preaching was perceived by one silversmith as a threat to the entire guild of idol-makers. He worried about unemployment because of this shift in consumer demand. He was not sure what could be done, and so he led a chant: "Great is Diana of the Ephesians." What effect that would have on the market was unclear. If potential buyers decided not to buy, what could the guild do about it? Customers were in control of their money. On its own authority, the guild had only this tactic: better preaching. A brief riot would solve nothing.

It was clear that the members of the guild would henceforth invest less in future production unless public opinion changed. Looking to the future, demand was likely to fall. Customers would bring negative sanctions against the guild. Lower sales would reduce market prices for the idols: greater supply than demand. These price signals would convey accurate information: falling demand. The economically rational response would be to reduce output. There would be layoffs in the industry. At least one guild member understood this.

3. Stone

The Roman state at this time did not move to call a halt to Paul's preaching. It would in AD 64.

In modern times, the guild would send its full-time team of lobbyists to Congress. These specialists in persuasion would invoke that most effective of all calls for economic intervention to save a contracting industry: reduced jobs. If the demand for any consumer good falls, and the industry is facing lower demand and lower profits, the industry warns voters that its demise would be a disaster for the job market. "Think of the jobs that will be lost if the government does not intervene immediately." Hazlitt began the chapter with these words:

> The lobbies of Congress are crowded with representatives of the X industry. The X industry is sick. The X industry is dying. It must be saved. It can be saved only by a tariff, by higher prices, or by a subsidy. If it is allowed to die, workers will be thrown on the streets. Their landlords, grocers, butchers, clothing stores, and local motion picture theaters will lose business, and depression will spread in ever-widening circles. But if the X industry, by prompt action of Congress, is saved—ah then! it will buy equipment from other industries; more men will be employed; they will give more business to the butchers, bakers, and neon-light makers, and then it is prosperity that will spread in ever-widening circles.

This strikes fear into the heart of any politician. Unemployed workers are far more likely to vote for his opponent in the next election. But the bureaucrat in Ephesus did not have to worry about that threat. Ephesians did not vote.

So, the politicians toss a stone through the window. It might be a restriction on competing industries. It might be a direct subsidy. But politicians do this in good faith: to save an industry that is "under attack."

Who is attacking it? Consumers. They are buying a rival's product. Or they are buying something else entirely.

4. Costs

The costs are the familiar ones: short-term unemployment in the industry, as capital shifts to those industries whose services are still in high demand. Investors will shift their capital. The price system will cease to convey accurate information regarding customers' preferences. But these price signals are the basis of consumers' control over what gets produced. Without the ability to impose such sanctions—positive and negative—they cannot retain control over producers. The intervention reduces the economic authority of consumers. It transfers authority to the politicians.

Then there are these costs: forfeited income for producers of services that customers prefer. They will not make profits. They will not purchase raw materials or build new production facilities. They will not hire workers.

There will be less innovation. The protected industry does not need to innovate in order to retain customers.

Taxpayers will lose if the subsidies come straight out of the national treasury. Hazlitt reminds us of cause and effect.

> This would be nothing more than a transfer of wealth or income to the X industry. The taxpayers would lose precisely as much as the people in the X industry gained. The great advantage of a subsidy, indeed, from the standpoint of the public, is that it makes this fact so clear. There is far less opportunity for the intellectual obfuscation that accompanies arguments for tariffs, minimum-price fixing, or monopolistic exclusion.

This transfer of wealth does not create wealth, he wrote.

> But the result of this subsidy is not merely that there has been a transfer of wealth or income, or that other

industries have shrunk in the aggregate as much as the X industry has expanded. The result is also (and this is where the net loss comes in to the nation considered as a unit) that capital and labor are driven out of industries in which they are more efficiently employed to be diverted to an industry in which they are less efficiently employed. Less wealth is created. The average standard of living is lowered compared with what it would have been.

The intervention does not merely equalize wealth. It lowers it.

There is this cost: a loss of faith in the principle of the rule of law. The new rule is this: success is penalized; failure is subsidized.

Then there is this: foreign producers will gain in international markets. The subsidized industry may not have to compete domestically, but it must compete internationally. It will lose its competitive edge. The influence of the industry will not reach its potential. New products, new production techniques, and new marketing techniques will give foreigners an advantage.

In this case, Hazlitt made a mistake. It is probably the biggest mistake in his book. He assumed that the subsidies are used to save dying industries. After all, this is the justification. In fact, the subsidies go to the most successful industries. These industries have the most political clout. For example, in the United States in 2010, about 1% of the Fortune 500 companies received over half of the federal subsidies: financial, utilities, telecommunications, oil, gas, and pipelines. In short, the official justification of these subsidies—saving W, X, Y, and Z industries—was in fact merely political cover. It was for the voters back home.

The wealth redistribution system is conducted in the name of helping the poor, the downtrodden, and the afflicted. It in fact subsidies the rich, the downtrodders (through politics) and the afflicters (through politics).

5. Consequences

There will be reduced economic growth. A token amount of this capital will remain invested in a contracting industry. Most of it will be invested in industries that are making lots of money, and which do not need the subsidies.

The U.S. government protected the American steel industry for decades. This was a huge industry. It was dominant in 1945. But foreign competition could not be kept out forever. Cheaper steel abroad provided a competitive edge for automobile imports, which were not equally protected. Employment in the automobile industry fell. Meanwhile, the steel industry is now a shell of what it was in 1950. Specialty steel companies are flourishing, but these are high-tech firms. They employ fewer workers than the old mills.

The classic example is the buggy whip industry. This example is easy to understand. But there was also the offal-sweeping industry. Automobiles and electric trolleys eliminated it by 1920.

Note: there were no federal subsidies to these industries. There were state and local subsidies to automobiles: tax-funded roads. There were municipal subsidies to trolleys until after World War II.

Subsidies are not given to save the X industry. Subsidies go to rivals of the X industry.

Conclusions

When you hear that X is a dying industry, ask yourself this: "Who is killing it?" There is a clear answer in a free market: consumers. But there may be another source: the state.

When politicians intervene to save a dying industry—a rare event—which means a contracting industry, they are announcing this: "We do not accept the decisions of consumers. We are substituting our judgment for their judgment." This is a conflict over authority: political authority vs. market authority. This is a debate about standards of institutional success: political vs. economic. The currency of the political realm is votes. The currency of the market realm is money.

Hazlitt's conclusion is on target:

> Paradoxical as it may seem to some, it is just as necessary to the health of a dynamic economy that dying industries be allowed to die as that growing industries be allowed to grow. The first process is essential to the second. It is as foolish to try to preserve obsolescent industries as to try to preserve obsolescent methods of production: this is often, in fact, merely two ways of describing the same thing. Improved methods of production must constantly supplant obsolete methods, if both old needs and new wants are to be filled by better commodities and better means.

There should be no subsidies to save a dying industry. Thankfully, there will not be many. The main problem is this: the huge subsidies to rich, well-connected industries.

Further Reading

For supporting material, go to bit.ly/CEIOL-Doc-14.

–15–

How the Price
System Works

*It is naught, it is naught, saith the buyer: but when he is
gone his way, then he boasteth (Proverbs 20:14).*

An alert reader will think: "Wait a minute. I've seen this
before." Indeed you have! And you will see it again: Chapters 16, 17, and 18. There is a valid reason for this. Hazlitt was
dealing with the same government policy in each chapter:
the policy of keeping prices higher than what the free market
would produce.

I began Chapter 13 with this verse. Chapter 13 is on parity prices: agricultural price floors that are set by the government rather than by competitive bidding in an open market.
In challenging the legitimacy of all price floors, I invoked the
free market's pricing system. I wrote the following:

> Every voluntary exchange involves buying and selling.
> The person who is called a buyer is a seller of money.
> He buys goods and services. The person who is called a
> seller is a buyer of money. He sells something of value
> to purchase money.

> The practice described here by Solomon is familiar. In
> negotiating, both the buyer of goods and the buyer of
> money complain that the asking price is too high. It is
> not a good enough deal. "It is naught, it is naught." Each
> hopes that the seller will drop his price. In the case of the
> buyer of money (seller of goods), he hopes that the buy-

er of goods (seller of money) will decide to take less for his money. Solomon knew that his listeners and readers would recognize this negotiating technique.

The technique rests on this institutional arrangement: the right to bid. We can see this in markets in which private property is secure (the window). We also see it in markets governed by politics (the stone).

In a society with a small retail market, where there are few rival options nearby, negotiation is basic to sales. In a highly developed economy, there is not much negotiation. We do not negotiate with a check-out clerk when we get to the front of the line at a supermarket. The clerk scans the bar code on the item's package, and the computer adds it to the list of items we are buying. The negotiation rule here is clear: "Take it or leave it." It is easy to leave it. Anyone can shop at a different store, or go online to check prices.

Sellers (buyers of money) bid against sellers. Buyers (sellers of money) bid against buyers. Out of this competitive bidding process—a gigantic auction system—come objective prices. There is little ignorance. Face-to-face negotiating is limited to zones of ignorance regarding prices and quality. *The better the information about market prices, the narrower the range for price negotiating.*

The best way to understand how the price system works is to understand an auction. The free market is a gigantic auction. All over the world, 24 hours a day, this auction is going on. Owners of money bid against each other to buy whatever they want to own or rent. Everyone with some asset to sell is an auctioneer. "Do I hear a higher bid?"

An auction is governed by this rule of asset allocation: *high bid wins.* So is the free market.

1. Owners

There are owners of scarce economic resources. What is a scarce resource? It is any resource for which, at zero price, there is greater demand than supply. This includes labor, which in turn includes mental labor: gathering information and exercising judgment.

There are also owners of money: the most marketable commodity. We call these people consumers, but they can also be investors.

Buyers of money (sellers of goods and services) want to obtain the highest money price possible, i.e., the obligation to deliver the least quantity of a crop. In contrast, buyers of goods and services (sellers of money) want to obtain more goods or services for whatever they are willing to pay.

There is a third aspect of ownership in a free market: *the legal right to bid.* This is another way of saying that owners possess the legal right to *disown* their property, whichever form of property they own: money or whatever money can buy.

2. Window

The window is all of the legal and institutional arrangements that produce what we call the free market. The free market is a system in which the ownership of goods and services is exchanged voluntarily. *Ownership is the right to disown legal titles to property.*

This right to disown does not include legal sovereignty, such as the right to vote or the right to sit on a jury. These are sometimes called *inalienable* rights, which means that they cannot be legally transferred. There is no legal market for them. *There is a difference between legal sovereignty and economic authority.* Economic authority is the right to sell what you own. For example, you do not have the right to sell your child because you do not own your child.

Buyers bid against buyers. Sellers bid against sellers. Out of this competitive bidding process comes an array of prices.

The money price of the latest asset exchange applies to all

of the assets in this category. If you buy one share of stock, this price applies to all other shares of that stock until there is another exchange at a different price. The marginal price—the latest price—sets the price for all of the other exchanges. These prices change constantly in highly developed markets.

This is why prices convey information to all active participants in a particular market. No one wants to pay more than he has to. The latest exchange price alerts all participants to whatever the terms of exchange have just been. *This was a market-clearing price.* No one was willing to pay more money to buy this asset, and no one was willing to sell for less.

Because this is a legally free market, the market for bidding is open to anyone who possesses money or assets that are for sale for money. Anyone who thinks that he has better information about the future price of an asset may put his money where his prediction is. He can legally make a bid to pay a higher price. This way, people are legally entitled to implement their plans in terms of their best estimates of what is coming next. They hope to profit. But in order to profit, they must make a bid that is then accepted. This exchange converts their subjective estimates of economic value into objective prices. This new selling price brings new information into the market. The participants are alerted to the fact that someone with either money (a buyer) or assets (a seller) thought that the previous array of prices was based on false information. Other bidders must now adjust their plans accordingly.

The free market allows an exchange of ownership. Those people who believe they possess better information than other owners and bidders can legally register their disagreement in an open market. "You're all wrong. I know better. I'll prove it to you. I'm bidding more."

Each exchange of ownership allocates scarce resources in a new way. Other participants who expect to profit in this market must now make decisions as to how best to allocate their resources: buy, sell, or hold. But holding means buying. The owner must defend his bid constantly. He remains the highest bidder for whatever it is he owns. He pays a price: forfeiting the ownership of whatever the highest rival bid is. "I won't sell it," he says. Then the would-be buyer responds: "Then you won't get what I just offered."

People bring to the marketplace their best estimates of what the future holds, asset by asset. They decide to buy, sell, or hold. Their individual decisions, either to bid or to refrain from bidding, establish objective prices in the market.

In short, the window is a gigantic auction.

3. Stone

People vote to elect politicians who then use the state to steal in the name of justice. Politicians use coercion to overturn the decisions of property owners who want to disown things in order to buy others.

Hazlitt never mentioned ethics in this book. Most free market economists also refuse to mention it. Yet legitimacy is always based in part on ethics. Any state that is perceived by the voters as being illegitimate will generate resistance. It will be forced to pay more to gain compliance. Its costs of operating will rise. It will attain fewer of its goals at yesterday's political prices.

Property owners whose plans are disrupted by the state's intervention into the free market are tempted to lose faith in the state, which refuses to defend the unified system of private ownership, disownership, and open bidding.

Agents of the civil government decide to control the price outcomes of the free market's auction process. They may decide to take steps to make some exchanges illegal. This reduces demand in a legal market. Or they may decide to enter this market as bidders on behalf of the government. This increases demand in a legal market. They alter the existing array of prices by means of their bids. They may even decide to set up a new system of rationing. All systems of economics are forms of rationing: asset allocation. There is rationing by government decree. There is also rationing by competitive bidding: prices.

Intervention sends a signal to other participants: "The economic conditions have changed. Demand is different." This information alters other participants' behavior. It changes their objective bids. Like a rock tossed into a pond, the government's participation in this market creates ripples. The array of prices that had existed in terms of the older conditions of supply and demand changes. People's behavior also changes in response to this new information.

Why do politicians interfere with auction prices? Because they think they can get more votes than they lose. They respond to what they perceive as new conditions of supply and demand for the currency of politics: votes.

Hazlitt blamed a single argument for this intervention: "Production for use is better than production for profit."

> It is on the fallacy of isolation, at bottom, that the "production-for-use-and-not-for-profit" school is based, with its attack on the allegedly vicious "price system." The problem of production, say the adherents of this school, is solved. (This resounding error, as we shall see, is also the starting point of most currency cranks and share-the-wealth charlatans.) The problem of production is solved. The scientists, the efficiency experts, the engineers, the technicians, have solved it. They could turn out almost anything you cared to mention in huge and practically unlimited amounts. But, alas, the world is not ruled by the engineers, thinking only of production, but by the businessmen, thinking only of profit. The businessmen give their orders to the engineers, instead of vice versa.

Critics of the free market adopted this argument during the Great Depression. We do not often hear it these days.

Another motivation for government economic planning is far stronger than people's belief in the "production for use" idea. This motivation is never stated this way in public, but it is a major root cause of all windows broken by the government. "The existing owners own more than I do. I want more. I can get more if the government takes over the system of distribution." This view is widely shared. It is an argument based on jealousy: benefiting at the expense of someone else, especially sellers.

Then there is this motivation. "The existing owners own more than I do. I can never own as much. Therefore, the government should be in charge of distributing property, even if I do not benefit. I may even lose. I don't care if I lose. The existing owners won't win." This is the argument from envy.

Hazlitt wrote:

> There are so many fallacies in this view that they cannot all be disentangled at once. But the central error, as we have hinted, comes from looking at only one industry, or even at several industries in turn, as if each of them existed in isolation. Each of them in fact exists in relation to all the others, and every important decision made in it is affected by and affects the decisions made in all the others.

This argument is Bastiat's. It is the broken window fallacy. The solution: follow the money. All of the money.

Hazlitt then turned to the division of labor to explain what prices do. Each worker produces something in terms of his specialized skills. Each wage earner achieves greater output this way, and therefore greater income. We exchange the output of our labor for the output of someone else's labor. We make bids. The result of our bidding is the extension of the auction process, which in turn is regulated through competitive prices. Hazlitt wrote: "Prices are fixed through the relationship of supply and demand, and in turn affect supply and demand." The more efficient producers make profits. The less efficient producers go out of business.

He also wrote: "Prices are determined by supply and demand, and demand is determined by how intensely people want a commodity and what they have to offer in exchange for it." This is true, but this has been understood ever since Adam Smith wrote *The Wealth of Nations* (1776). But the existence of government intervention and allocation indicates that lots of voters either do not believe Smith or else they do not care (envy).

4. Costs

The highest costs of government intervention into the market process are ethical costs. Most people who believe in private property recognize that the state has become immoral when it uses coercion to intervene into market exchanges. They see that the politicians have adopted this commandment: "Thou shalt not steal, except by majority vote." Economists rarely talk about this ethical cost as the number-one cost of state intervention. They prefer to pretend that they are value-free analysts. They are not. They are merely analysts who do not believe in permanent ethical standards, especially ethical standards to which are attached predictable institutional sanctions: positive and negative.

Economists also do not discuss the judicial principle that undergirds the concept of private property: *the link between ownership and personal responsibility*. Men are responsible before God judicially. They are also responsible before other bidders economically. A man who says "I will not sell" necessarily also says: "I will retain full responsibility for my ownership." Other bidders say this by their bids: "I can do a better job as an owner." The man who refuses to sell necessarily pays a price to retain ownership: whatever the highest bidder would have handed over to him. The free market's pricing system forces each owner to pay the price of refusing to sell. Therefore, *judicial responsibility is reinforced economically*.

There are other costs of state intervention. The main ones have to do with undermining the authority of consumers (customers) to shape the behavior of producers. Consumers reward some producers by buying. They also penalize other producers by not buying. State interference with market pricing disrupts the auction process. This intervention reduces the ability of consumers to persuade producers to do things the consumers' way. Producers pay attention to the government's most recent rules or the government's most recent bids, and also its promises of future bids. Sellers honor this auction principle: "High bid wins." When the state offers the highest bid, it wins. But then someone inescapably must lose: the taxpayer.

Hazlitt repeated an argument he had used in Chapter 14: "Saving the X Industry."

> It follows that it is just as essential for the health of a dynamic economy that dying industries should be allowed to die as that growing industries should be allowed to grow. For the dying industries absorb labor and capital that should be released for the growing industries.

The government saves one industry at the expense of other industries. It does so by stealing from one group of consumers in order to transfer the loot to another group of consumers —minus handling fees, of course. "There's no such thing as a free thief." If you use an armed thug as your middleman, he will demand payment.

5. Consequences

The main consequences of the state's interference with the price system have been constant calls politically for the government to intervene again. Part of this is the desire of members of other special-interest groups to get in on the deal. Free money or free goods are always politically popular.

More insidious is what Ludwig von Mises described in his 1951 speech, "The Middle of the Road Policy Leads to Socialism." The state's intervention disrupts production. It disrupts the market's auction process that directs production. These disruptions cause losses for some groups. They complain about these ill effects. So, the policy makers in the government intervene again in order to repair the visible damage that its previous intervention produced. This creates another series of negative side effects. Every time the state intervenes to clean up the mess it has produced, the mess spreads.

This brings us back to the issue of the famous *law of unintended consequences*. It can be summarized as follows: "There are no side effects. There are only effects. We use the phrase 'side effects' to describe effects that we do not like."

When Western Europe went off the government-guaranteed gold coin standard in the fall of 1914 at the beginning of World War I, it became possible for national governments to interfere with pricing on a scale that had not been seen since the days of the Pharaohs of Egypt. This intervention led to a series of boom-bust cycles that Mises had predicted in his 1912 book, *The Theory of Money and Credit*. The expansion of central banking, which he had warned about, made the booms bigger and the busts deeper.

Government intervention into the price system grew worse during World War II: rationing. That war ended for Americans in August 1945. Public opinion regarding government intervention and rationing had begun to decline in the year that Hazlitt's book was published. The Truman administration was forced politically to abandon most price controls by the end of 1946.

Only in Nixon's two years of price controls, 1971–73, did the United States again deal with full-scale price and wage controls. Nixon unilaterally abandoned the last legal traces of the old gold standard on the same day that he announced price and wage controls: August 15, 1971. He "closed the gold window" by prohibiting foreign governments and central banks from buying gold from the U.S. Treasury at $35 an ounce. The great peacetime price inflation began immediately. It lasted for over a decade.

Federal spending as a percentage of GDP has increased, due to increased debt, but federal revenues as a percentage of GDP have never reached the level of 1945. Even then, the ratio was only slightly above 20%. It is now slightly below. The American public resists increased taxes. Lobbyists who lobby Congress make sure that the super-rich pay a lower percentage than the middle class does. But in the area of federal debt, the process of political over-promising has escalated throughout the West. These promises cannot be fulfilled. Either there will be massive tax hikes or a Great Default. I think the latter is more likely.

Conclusions

The call for government intervention into market pricing is ancient. This call was resisted politically in the West until the decade before World War I began. After that war ended in 1918, the West saw the triumph of the isms: Communism, Fascism, National Socialism, Fabianism, and the smaller isms that arose in the wake of the larger isms.

Calls for government intervention into the price system have multiplied. Hazlitt's book dealt with lots of these calls. But these calls have played second fiddle in the West to three government-bankrupting ideas: government pensions, government health care for the aged, and military empire. Europe is further along the path to bankruptcy because of the first two programs, along with government health care for the whole population. The United States has specialized in war since 1946.

Because of the price-disrupting effects of central banking and fractional reserve banking—both of which are government-licensed monopolies—the state's interventions in these closely related sectors of the economy have subsidized the allocation of capital away from what consumers would have chosen, had politically favored special-interest groups not been furnished with fiat money. The economy of the world is now addicted to monetary inflation. Among modern economists, Austrian School economic analysis alone focuses on these disrupting effects. This outlook is not known by the public, and it is rejected by academic economists. Thus, the West is headed for the Great Default.

The window is cracked. The shattering is still ahead of us.

Further Reading

For supporting material, go to bit.ly/CEIOL-Doc-15.

–16–

"Stabilizing" Commodities

It is naught, it is naught, saith the buyer: but when he is gone his way, then he boasteth (Proverbs 20:14).

This chapter deals with the same issue that Chapter 13 did and Chapter 15 did: government intervention into the economy to keep commodity prices from falling. Such a policy favors existing producers at the expense of consumers.

Politicians dare not admit to voters what they are really doing—supporting existing producers—and why: campaign contributions. Remember: the beneficiaries of special-interest legislation are self-interested to a fault. The victims—customers who are voters—may never have heard of the policy, nor would they be interested if they did hear about it. The political system is asymmetric. The beneficiaries of political pressure have better information and greater motivation to rig the system in their favor than the voters do. The beneficiaries are highly focused. They persuade politicians to re-direct the taxpayers' money in their direction. The voters do not follow the money. The politicians and the special-interest groups understand this.

1. Owners

This is a recapitulation of my arguments in Chapter 13. There are several groups of owners, as always.

One group owns money, which is the most marketable commodity. Economists classify these people under the classification of consumers. They are sellers of money and buyers of goods to consume.

Another group is made up of owners of natural resources—in this case, commodities. Economists classify natural resources under the general category of land.

There are other owners. They own commodities, but only temporarily. They are intermediaries in between landowners and final consumers. They are producers. They purchase raw materials, labor services, and buy or rent capital in order to transform raw materials into final products. Producers are not final consumers. They are buyers, but they are also sellers. They buy in order to make a profit: buy low, sell high. They can be classified under the category of customers.

There may be a fourth group: retailers. They buy goods that contain restructured commodities. They sell these to consumers. They own these commodities temporarily.

There is a fifth group: owners of forecasts regarding the future. They may be able to sell this information. They may choose to give it away. Until this subjective information affects actual bids in the marketplace, it is irrelevant to the pricing system. But whenever these people put their money where their forecasts are, by buying or selling commodity futures contracts, they become speculators. Their bids affect prices at the margin: up or down.

Because owners have the right to own, they also have the right to disown what they own. They can legally sell. They can legally make an exchange. This brings us to the window.

2. Window

This is a recapitulation of my arguments in Chapter 13.

Consumers compete against consumers. Producers compete against producers. Raw materials owners compete against raw materials owners. Owners of capital compete against owners of capital. Commodity futures speculators compete against each other: "longs" vs. "shorts." **Out of this bidding process comes an array of prices**. The economic order in a free market system is based on a series of auctions. The same rule of exchange governs all of them: "High bid wins."

The average person knows what an auction is. He understands why the high bid wins: to decide who buys it without creating dissension. He understands that bidders compete against bidders. But a free market economist has a major educational task: to persuade the general public that the orderliness and fairness of an auction is a legitimate model for the entire economy. The principle of open bidding produces an equally orderly and equally fair economy. The ability to make this application of logic—from a local auction to an international auction—is a limited resource. This is demonstrated by over two centuries of resistance to the idea of free trade, which is most famously argued in Adam Smith's *Wealth of Nations* (1776).

The average person can easily understand and readily approve of the allocation principle of "high bid wins" at an auction. One of the tasks I have set for myself in writing this book is to help readers make the conceptual transition from "high bid wins" at a local auction to "high bid wins" for every transaction. This is more easily said than done.

In the auction markets (plural) for commodities, the principle of "high bid wins" benefits those buyers and sellers who come to an agreement on a price. There are multiple sub-markets in this and every other market. The initial market is established between commodity owners and producers. The second phase of the market is established between producers and middlemen: retailers. The final stage is the transaction between retailers and consumers. At every step, the rule is "high bid wins."

This principle of distribution annoys those who do not make the highest bid. Sometimes this annoys them so much that they form a political action group that campaigns for legislation that restricts the use of "high bid wins." People who ran out of money before the auction was over demand that the state impose legal price ceilings. But high bids come on both sides of a transaction. Sometimes those sellers of commodities who were forced to take too low a price, and who dropped out of the auction in order to avoid a loss, see an opportunity. They may be able to persuade the government to make lower bids illegal. This leads us to this chapter's stone.

3. Stone

The government intervenes to create a price floor for a commodity. Politicians declare that prices have become too volatile. The public hears the word "volatile," and thinks: "Prices get too high. Then they get too low. This is not orderly. We need orderly prices. The government is going to stabilize prices." This is what the politicians actually say in defense of their actions. But what they really mean by "volatile prices" is this: "Prices are consistently too low to sustain high profits for one of our major special-interest business groups." Hazlitt summarized the politicians' official defense of price floor intervention.

> They have no wish, they declare, to raise the price of commodity X permanently above its natural level. That, they concede, would be unfair to consumers. But it is *now* obviously selling far *below* its natural level. The producers cannot make a living. Unless we act promptly, they will be thrown out of business. Then there will be a real scarcity, and consumers will have to pay exorbitant prices for the commodity. The apparent bargains that the consumers are now getting will cost them dear in the end. For the present "temporary" low price cannot last. But we cannot afford to wait for so-called natural market forces, or for the "blind" law of supply and demand, to correct the situation. For by that time the producers will be ruined and a great scarcity will be upon us. The government must *act*. All that we really want to do is to correct these violent, senseless *fluctuations* in price. We are not trying to *boost* the price; we are only trying to *stabilize* it.

How can the government do this? Hazlitt offered this example. One way is to lend farmers money so they can hold crops off the market. This is true, but this is simply recapitulating what he wrote in Chapter 13 on parity prices. He then repeated other farm subsidy arguments. This takes the remainder of Section 1 and all of Section 2.

While his chapter is fairly long, Hazlitt offered no other example of a program like parity prices for agriculture. There was a reason for this. There was no other program like it. In early 1946, price ceilings were still in force. Producers could sell everything they offered for sale. Their problem was government rationing, not a lack of demand. There were major shortages of everything that had a price ceiling imposed by the government. This is why this chapter was theoretical rather than a description of existing policies.

There was another major example of common price regulation in the name of combating price volatility: the gold standard. The U.S. government bought all of the gold offered to it. After 1933, it forbade Americans from buying gold for monetary purposes: a rigged market. It paid a specific price for gold, beginning in 1934: $35 per ounce. It had a huge stockpile of gold in early 1946—the largest in the world. That gold exchange standard—no coins, no legal ownership by Americans—was the weakened remnant of the 1933 gold coin standard. But Hazlitt did not discuss the gold standard in this chapter.

He was trapped by his own economic logic. He was a defender of the 1946 version of the gold standard, although he would have preferred the 1932 version. Yet, in terms of his economic analysis in this chapter, the gold standard had always been a price-rigging system—one that pre-dated the Agricultural Adjustment Administration by a century. It was anti-free market, according to this chapter. It was just another government-rigged price floor system. The American gold standard, because it involved a government guarantee to buy gold at a fixed price per ounce, had always violated the auction principle of "no rigged bottom bids." This is the inevitable implication of a government-guaranteed gold standard. It is one more government intervention into the free market. It no longer exists anywhere on earth. The old gold coin standard was used to buy the gold of the people. Then all of the governments stole the people's gold. They all violated their promises to redeem paper money for a specific quantity of gold, including gold coins. The governments all did what governments do best: deceive the voters while stealing from them.

4. Costs

There will be higher prices for consumers under this kind of price floor system. This is the reason why politicians voted for the intervention. This is what the special-interest group wanted. Hazlitt then applied the logic of Bastiat once again. The consumers lose. So do the producers and retailers of the goods they would have preferred to buy.

> But, as a result of the lower price, they will have money left over, which they did not have before, to spend on other things. The consumers, therefore, will obviously be better off. But their increased spending in other directions will give increased employment in other lines, which will then absorb the former marginal farmers in occupations in which their efforts will be more lucrative and more efficient.

The losers in business are those who are more efficient than the businesses that could not compete at the previously lower prices.

> A uniform proportional restriction (to return to our government intervention scheme) means, on the one hand, that the efficient low-cost producers are not permitted to turn out all the output they can at a low price. It means, on the other hand, that the inefficient

high-cost producers are artificially kept in business. This increases the average cost of producing the product. It is being produced less efficiently than otherwise. The inefficient marginal producer thus artificially kept in that line of production continues to tie up land, labor, and capital that could much more profitably and efficiently be devoted to other uses.

There are winners: higher-cost producers. The losers are these: (1) all consumers of these commodities, who pay higher prices; (2) the most efficient producers of these commodities; (3) the producers of the goods that consumers would have bought, but did not because of high prices in one sector of the economy. Thus, there is a net loss of wealth in the community. This was Hazlitt's conclusion. It is also my conclusion. But it is not the conclusion of most voters. It may or may not be the conclusion of politicians. Members of the favored special-interest groups may not understand, but any economist on the organization's payroll does understand. He is paid well to mislead the public about the nature of the arrangement.

Hazlitt was a nice fellow. He avoided following the loot all the way to hired economists' salaries. I am not that nice.

5. Consequences

Hazlitt feared the creation of an international body that would act as a political agent of commodity producers.

Of course the international commodity controls that are being proposed now, we are told, are going to avoid all these errors. This time prices are going to be fixed that are "fair" not only for producers but for consumers. Producing and consuming nations are going to agree on just what these fair prices are, because no one will be unreasonable. Fixed prices will necessarily involve "just" allotments and allocations for production and consumption as among nations, but only cynics will anticipate any unseemly international disputes regarding these. Finally, by the greatest miracle of all, this postwar world of superinternational controls and coercions is also going to be a world of "free" international trade!

Here, he was dead wrong. He did not understand the long-run agenda of what is sometimes called the New World Order. Its goal, beginning in the early 1920's, was to create managed international trade, with low tariffs. This would bankrupt domestic industries.

The goal from the beginning was to create an international political order that would be marked by tariffs against non-member nations, and a low-tariff free trade zone inside the international confederacy. This plan was initially tested in the United States, beginning in 1786. James Madison came up with the plan for the Annapolis Convention in 1786, steered it through the Constitutional Convention in 1787, and got it ratified by state ratification conventions in 1787-88. His political goal was to replace the decentralized Articles of Confederation with a new constitution that centralized political power. He initially promoted this in 1786 as a way to increase trade among colonies.

This two-stage strategy—economics (open agenda) to politics (concealed agenda)—was imitated next by German nationalists. They got treaties signed by German principalities in 1833: a customs union. It abolished tariffs internally, but it imposed them on imports. The new system began on January 1, 1834: the *Zollverein.* Political unification followed in 1871.

Immediately after World War I, the same political agenda began to be formulated by a French bureaucrat, Jean Monnet, and his supporters behind the scene. At the 1919 peace conference at Versailles, Monnet worked closely with John D. Rockefeller's long-term agent, Raymond Fosdick. They and their financial supporters wanted to create a centrally managed international order. That plan failed when the U.S. Senate refused to ratify the League of Nations treaty in 1920. Fosdick returned home from France in 1920 to take over the Rockefeller Foundation, which he ran for the next 28 years.

The New World Order's plans for regional political consolidation were not begun in the inter-war years, but funding laid the conceptual foundations of the economic side of the program. The Rockefeller Foundation was active in this work. It put up money for academic conferences on industrial and agricultural protectionism, beginning in 1936. It co-funded free trade economist Wilhelm Röpke. He discussed this funding in the Preface to his book, *International Economic Disintegration* (1942). The internationalists' political agenda began after the end of after World War II in 1945. The first step was the 1951 treaty that established the European Economic Coal and Steel Community. The process continued, treaty by treaty. It was completed by the European Union in 1994–2004.

The main exceptions to this system in Europe are farmers, especially French farmers. But with the exception of agriculture, the trend has been toward lower tariffs, more trade, and lower commodity prices. Manufacturing benefits from lower commodity prices.

Here was the bait: international economic integration through low or no tariffs, but with non-elected bureaucratic managers of the rules. Then there was the switch: political unification. Economic benefits—low tariffs, greater wealth— served as the lure that baited the political trap. In order to gain the economic benefits of greater trade, we are assured by proponents of bureaucratically managed trade, nations must surrender much of their political sovereignty. Yet from the point of view of economic analysis, this call for political unification is a conceptual error. It confuses economic authority with judicial sovereignty. Any nation can gain the benefits of free trade simply by unilaterally lowering its tariffs. There is no necessity of surrendering national political sovereignty to an international political entity.

Hazlitt did not see this bait-and-switch operation in 1946.

He therefore failed to see what was coming next: not commodity price stabilization by price floors, but rather reduced tariffs and high profits for highly efficient multinational firms, which are behind the New World Order.

Conclusions

The desire of national cartels is restricted entry, high tariffs, and high prices. The only large-scale national cartel to achieve this in the United States is the agricultural cartel. The model is the sugar cartel, which extends back to the 1790's.

Raw commodities are part of an international market. Low tariffs on non-agricultural raw commodities have predominated in the United States. This low-tariff system has led to an extensive increase in the foreign trade component of the American economy. Foreign trade accelerated after 1970 because of reduced tariffs on most finished products. American consumers have benefited. But politically, they have been pushed in the direction of international economic treaties. The main one is NAFTA: the North American Free Trade Agreement (1994). Others have been proposed. They will probably be imposed on the voters.

Further Reading

For supporting material, go to bit.ly/CEIOL-Doc-16.

Government Price-Fixing

It is naught, it is naught, saith the buyer: but when he is gone his way, then he boasteth (Proverbs 20:14).

Once again, Hazlitt returned to the issue of government price fixing. In Chapters 13, 15, and 16, this price fixing was in the form of price floors. In this chapter, he dealt with price ceilings. But the theoretical issue is the same in all of these chapters: the state's interference with the price system, a system that rests on two legal principles: (1) private ownership, which includes the right to disown property, and (2) the right to make a bid for ownership. By "right," I mean an individual's ability to make a transaction, or to refuse to make a transaction, in a legal system that preserves *the right to exclude*. So did Hazlitt.

Hazlitt wrote that governments resort to price ceilings during wartime. In early 1946, the United States was just coming out of four years of price and wage ceilings. The transition was not yet complete when he wrote his book.

1. Owners

Members of one group of owners have legal title to property. This includes their labor, which they can rent. Because these owners have legal title, they have the right to transfer this legal title: to disown something. We call this act of disownership *selling*.

Members of another group of owners have legal title to money: the most marketable commodity. They also have the right to disown money. We call this act of disownership *buying*.

2. Window

We have covered this repeatedly in earlier chapters. Buyers of money (sellers of services) seek out sellers of money (buyers of services). The market is a complex institutional arrangement that is the product of years of exchanges. These exchanges have been based on private ownership. Legal and customary arrangements have established an individual's legal right to buy and sell without the threat of coercion, including coercion by authorized agents of the state.

Prices have developed over periods of time. These are not fixed by law, but they are familiar to participants. Prices convey valuable information to participants. Prices makes their decision-making more accurate. People can more easily count the costs of their decisions, past, present, and future. Prices fluctuate, but normally they do not fluctuate much. This stability reduces the costs of transactions. Past prices do not guarantee future prices, but they do point to a pattern. They bid down money prices. When prices get comparatively high, sellers enter the market to sell. When prices get comparatively low, buyers enter the market to buy. They bid up money prices.

Final buyers are the sources of market pricing. They possess the most marketable commodity: money. They compete against other buyers. The free market is an auction, both in theory and practice.

Entrepreneurs who buy production goods and services try to guess what final buyers will pay and in what quantities, but no one knows. Good guesses produce profits. Bad guesses produce losses. Final buyers retain control over production and distribution by means of their bids. High bids win.

3. Stone

The state enters the scene. Politicians are told by voters that certain prices are too high. Sellers are gouging buyers, buyers say. Buyers do not tell politicians: "We buyers are driving up prices. Stop us before we spend again!" No, they blame sellers, who are simply responding to the highest bids, sale by sale.

Politicians pass laws against raising prices. These laws impose what are called price ceilings. This is what most people have in mind when they think, "price controls."

Voters do not understand this economic law: *There are no price controls. There are only people controls.* People bid to buy. A price control law makes it illegal for a seller to complete the transaction. Buyers make bids above the price ceiling, but sellers who do not want to be arrested resist the temptation to sell, at least in the legal markets.

Hazlitt described the argument of voters who want these people controls. They want to control the rich.

> The argument for holding down the price of these goods will run something like this. If we leave beef (let us say) to the mercies of the free market, the price will be pushed up by competitive bidding so that only the rich will get it. People will get beef not in proportion to their need, but only in proportion to their purchasing power. If we keep the price down, everyone will get his fair share.

There is an implied ethical argument: fairness. "The government must force bidders to be fair. The high bidders should be compelled by law to cease bidding against people with less money."

What price is fair? What criteria of fairness will bureaucrats who enforce these laws use as guidelines? If the politicians do not fix all prices, then the list of retail price ceilings will be in the billions. Not millions—billions. There are that many products in the United States. This does not count services.

4. Costs

The reason why a price ceiling is demanded by voters is that too many bidders are bidding at the auction. The voters want this stopped. But the problem still remains: Who should be allowed by the bureaucrats to buy? There is greater demand than supply at the artificially low price. Instead of the top bidder who goes home with the item, there are half a dozen bidders who can still afford to bid, and who still want to bid. Five of them must be turned away. On what legal basis? More to the point, on what moral basis? What is fair? Will the five non-buyers agree on this standard? Will they agree with the bureaucrat's decision in applying it?

There is now growing resentment among excluded bidders. There may be conflict if this allocation procedure continues.

When the war ends, disappointed buyers can no longer be dismissed with this phrase, universal in World War II: "Don't you know there's a war on?"

Under price ceilings, consumers lose their control over the production process, which is the flip side of the distribution process. Power increasingly flows toward the government and its enforcement agents. It flows away from consumers.

The effect of a price ceiling is a shortage: more demand than supply at the fixed price. The government must then ration by some methodology other than price.

The price control program spreads. Mises said why in his 1951 lecture: "The Middle of the Road Policy Leads to Socialism." New rules are passed in order to fix the disruptions of the previous interventions. Hazlitt described this process.

> But as the government extends this price-fixing backwards, it extends at the same time the consequences that originally drove it to this course. Assuming that it has the courage to fix these costs, and is able to enforce its decisions, then it merely, in turn, creates shortages of the various factors—labor, feedstuffs, wheat, or whatever—that enter into the production of the final commodities. Thus the government is driven to controls in ever-widening circles, and the final consequence will be the same as that of universal price-fixing.

The trend is clear: what Hayek in 1944 called the road to serfdom.

> The natural consequence of a thoroughgoing overall price control which seeks to perpetuate a given historic price level, in brief, must ultimately be a completely regimented economy. Wages would have to be held down as rigidly as prices. Labor would have to be rationed as ruthlessly as raw materials. The end result would be that the government would not only tell each consumer precisely how much of each commodity he could have; it would tell each manufacturer precisely what quantity of each raw material he could have and what quantity of labor. Competitive bidding for workers could no more be tolerated than competitive bidding for materials. The result would be a petrified totalitarian economy, with every business firm and every worker at the mercy of the government, and with a final abandonment of all the traditional liberties we have known.

5. Consequences.

Under price ceiling, bidding is illegal. Prices no longer convey accurate information about supply and demand. Output falls. Economic growth falls or disappears. Rationing spreads. Shortages increase.

Of course, none of this happens if the central bank deflates. But they rarely do.

The West did not march down the road to serfdom after World War II. Before 1946 was over, a strike by beef producers forced President Truman to remove all price controls on beef. That was the end of most of the national controls.

The American public got tired of the shortages. They got tired of the rationing coupons. They wanted to return to the world of 1941.

In Great Britain, the Labour Party won the 1945 election.

They kept the price controls in place until 1951. Shortages were universal. So was rationing. There were controls in the Western zone of Germany until the economics minister Ludwig Erhard abolished them on June 20, 1948. The German economic recovery began the next day.

The public did not know that price controls led to rationing. But the voters wanted an end to rationing. This forced the hand of the governments. They had to abolish the controls. This is why periods of price and wage controls in peacetime do not last long. Voters will not tolerate rationing, except in limited markets.

Nixon imposed price and wage controls by fiat on August 15, 1971, the day he abolished the gold-exchange standard. The controls created bottlenecks, visible in long lines at gasoline stations. They were abolished in April 1974.

Conclusions

Price and wage controls have come and gone in history. They do not last long. Black markets undermine them: goods and services flow into these illegal markets. Government rationing creates resistance politically. The public does not understand the logic of price ceilings, but they recognize the government's response: rationing. Voters will not tolerate this in peacetime. Their answer is this: "Don't you know there's not a war on?"

Further Reading

For supporting material, go to bit.ly/CEIOL-Doc-17.

–18–

Minimum Wage Laws

It is naught, it is naught, saith the buyer: but when he is gone his way, then he boasteth (Proverbs 20:14).

Once again, Hazlitt returned to the issue of government price fixing. In Chapters 13, 15, and 16, this price fixing was in the form of price floors. It is in this chapter, too.

A minimum wage law is a government-mandated price floor on labor services. It does not apply to machines. It does not apply to computer programs. So, to the extent that a machine or a computer program can perform labor services at a cost per hour lower than the minimum wage, to that extent the law is unenforceable.

1. Owners

One set of owners possess money: business owners. They may also possess capital equipment, which includes land and buildings. They possess business plans. These plans involve hiring human laborers.

Another set of owners possess the ability to deliver labor services. These people are eligible to rent out these services.

A third set of owners will decide at some point whether to purchase goods and services that have been produced by a combination of business capital and labor services. They will determine retroactively which sellers prosper and which do not.

The key fact of ownership is personal responsibility. God holds owners responsible, because He is the original owner. These individuals are His stewards.

2. Window

The window is a product of a society's moral, legal, and cultural traditions and institutions. It is known as the free market. Those with money to spend work out arrangements with people who want to sell goods to buyers, i.e., spenders of money.

In this system, people who hire workers seek to locate people who rent out these services at some price. Economic exchange always depends on an agreed-upon price. Buyers compete against buyers. Sellers compete against sellers. Only in the final stage of the hiring process does face-to-face bargaining take place: would-be employer vs. would-be employee. The prospective employer does not know how little money the prospective employee will accept, and the prospective employee does not know how much money the prospective employer will pay. In this zone of ignorance, there may be negotiating. But probably not. Time is not a free resource. Employers usually make this offer to entry-level workers: "Take it or leave it. I am too busy to negotiate."

The employer acts as an economic agent of future customers. He will give them an opportunity to buy the output of his production process. The employer also acts as an economic agent of his employees. In order to earn money, employees must sell their services to customers. The employees do not know how to market their services directly to customers, but the employer believes that he does. So confident is the employer that he is willing to pay money to the employees to perform certain tasks, irrespective of the near-term decisions of customers. The business pays these employees until the lack of customers makes it evident to the employer that he has misjudged customer demand. Only then will he fire some or all of his employees.

The wage is a signal to other workers and other employers regarding the prevailing conditions of supply and demand. If this wage is a market-clearing wage, there will be no rival workers offering to work for a lower wage for the same job, and there will be no rival employers offering to pay more.

3. Stone

Members of trade unions face a major problem when workers are willing to work for wages lower than those preferred by the members. These union members cannot find enough employers who will pay them above-market wages, i.e., wages at which employers can hire all the employees they want to hire. The members see a way to reduce competition from low-wage workers: get the government to pass a law making it illegal for employers to pay wages below a minimum. This way, union members may find employers who will pay them above-market wages.

In the year that the first federal minimum wage law was passed, 1938, union members who lived in the North faced competition from manufacturers located in the South, where wages were lower. They preferred not to face this competition. Northern manufacturers were happy to support a minimum wage that was lower than what they paid, but which was higher than what manufacturers in the South paid.

To gain their votes, Northern union members and Northern manufacturers told their representatives in Congress that Congress had to pass a minimum wage law. Beginning in 1938 and ever since, Congress has done exactly that.

Politicians who respond to this political pressure are in need of an acceptable political justification for such a law. There is one that has been used for decades: the workers' need for a living wage. If taken literally, the phrase makes no economic sense. People do not voluntarily accept wages that will not sustain life—at least not for long. That is because such workers soon die. Their deaths reduce the supply of surviving people who are willing to work for a non-living wage. When the supply of labor falls, market wages rise, other things being equal. So, the phrase "living wage" is a political slogan, not an economic phenomenon. The phrase means this: *a wage that is above the wage that other workers are ready to accept, but who are prohibited by the minimum wage law from accepting.*

4. Costs

The market no longer clears at the new, higher wage. This means that more workers offer to work at this higher wage than there are offers to hire them. The wage floor creates a glut of labor offers. This is the result of all price floors: more suppliers than buyers. Those workers who offer to work are disappointed. They must seek work elsewhere. Hazlitt described this situation.

> The first thing that happens, for example, when a law is passed that no one shall be paid less than $30 for a forty-hour week is that no one who is not worth $30 a week to an employer will be employed at all. You cannot make a man worth a given amount by making it illegal for anyone to offer him anything less. You merely deprive him of the right to earn the amount that his abilities and situation would permit him to earn, while you deprive the community even of the moderate services that he is capable of rendering. In brief, for a low wage you substitute unemployment. You do harm all around, with no comparable compensation.

This situation is a benefit to those workers who have jobs, but only for as long as their employers do not find labor-saving equipment to replace them. They no longer face competition from human beings who are willing to work for less.

It is also a benefit to employers who are willing to break the law. They are now able to find able-bodied workers who are willing to work below the minimum wage—well below. The supply of unemployed workers has increased. They must take job offers that they would have rejected before the minimum wage law went into effect.

The major losers of minimum wages in the United States are black teenage males with minimal job skills. They are less desirable employees. They live in parts of town that are poverty-stricken. They cannot afford to drive to a part of town where there may be job offers at the minimum wage. Their one tool of employment in their neighborhoods is their willingness to work at a below-market wage. This way, they can gain the experience and skills required to get better job offers. But it is now illegal for employers to accept such offers. Thus, when the minimum wage was raised significantly above entry-level wages in 1961 in the first year of Kennedy's presidency, the unemployment rate for black teenage males rose above the rate for white teenage males and everyone else. It has never come down to match other groups' unemployment rates. Prior to 1961, black teenage males had a lower unemployment rate than white teenage males.

These young males are ready recruits for gangs. The crime rate rises in inner cities. The main perpetrators are black teenage males and unmarried young men.

5. Consequences

Basic to economic growth are entry-level jobs for teenagers. Here is where they gain the skills they need. Small local businesses are the usual employers. But this avenue for young people without formal educational certification is cut off by minimum wage laws. This works against small businesses, especially business start-ups, which are the primary sources of job creation.

Ever since the early 1960's in the United States, the black underclass has remained a constant social problem. They never enter the legal labor markets. Wherever there are minimum wage laws, there is an underclass filled with young men who are never integrated into the community of married, employed heads of households. Crime is far above average in these groups. These men do not become productive members of their communities.

There is then political pressure for the state to intervene and create welfare programs to support these men and the women they do not marry. Inter-generational welfare lures these people into lives of dependency on the state.

Conclusions

The minimum wage law is one more state intervention into the market of voluntary exchange: of ownership and its concomitant implication, disownership. It rests on the idea that people must not be allowed to make arrangements with each other that they see as beneficial—better than the status quo. Politicians and bureaucrats who are distant from the circumstances facing people locally establish the legal terms of exchange for labor services.

The people who have the best information about local employment opportunities are prohibited from pursuing opportunities to improve their conditions. These same people with the greatest motivation to improve their conditions are told by the local agents of distant politicians that they are not allowed to pursue any avenue of improvement at a wage below the national minimum.

The substitution of labor-saving machinery has accelerated since the early 1980's. Today, the rapid development of computerized operations and robotics is threatening low-skilled laborers as never before. The costs associated with replacing human labor are now falling at an exponential rate, and have been ever since the development of the first commercial microcomputers in 1978. This makes the effects of a minimum wage law even more devastating for entry-level workers and older workers with minimum skills. The minimum wage law subsidizes this substitution effect.

Once again, we see that the state's intervention into the free market, in the name of the poor and the downtrodden, has increased the percentage of the poor and the downtrodden. The victims are poorer and more trodden down than they would have been. But in the case of the minimum wage law, it has raised crime, too. People in inner cities bear the brunt of the costs.

Further Reading

For supporting material, go to bit.ly/CEIOL-Doc-18.

Do Unions Really
Raise Wages?

*It is naught, it is naught, saith the buyer: but when he is
gone his way, then he boasteth (Proverbs 20:14).*

Once again, Hazlitt returned to the issue of government
price fixing. In Chapters 13, 15, 16, and 18 price fixing
was in the form of price floors. It is in this chapter, too.

This may not be seen initially as a case of government
price-fixing. By the end of this chapter, I hope you will see that
it is entirely a case of government price fixing. It is one more
example of a price floor.

1. Owners

One set of owners possess money: business owners. They
may also possess capital equipment, which includes land and
buildings. They possess business plans. These plans involve
hiring human laborers.

Another set of owners possess the ability to deliver labor
services. These people are eligible to rent out these services.

A third set of owners will decide at some point whether to
purchase goods and services that have been produced by a
combination of business capital and labor services. They will
determine retroactively which sellers prosper and which do not.

All participants possess the legal right to bid.

2. Window

The window is a product of a society's moral, legal, and cultural traditions and institutions. It is known as the free market.

Those with money to spend work out arrangements with people who want to sell goods to buyers, i.e., spenders of money.

In this system, people who hire workers seek to locate people who rent out these services at some price. Economic exchange always depends on an agreed-upon price. Buyers compete against buyers. Sellers compete against sellers. Only in the final stage of the hiring process does face-to-face bargaining take place: would-be employer vs. would-be employee. The prospective employer does not know how little money the prospective employee will accept, and the prospective employee does not know how much money the prospective employer will pay. In this zone of ignorance, there may be negotiating. But probably not. Time is not a free resource. Employers usually make this offer: "Take it or leave it. I am too busy to negotiate."

The employer acts as an economic agent of future customers. He will give them an opportunity to buy the output of his production process. The employer also acts as an economic agent of his employees. In order to earn money, employees must sell their services to customers. The employees do not know how to market their services directly to customers, but the employer believes that he does. So confident is the employer that he is willing to pay money to the employees to perform certain tasks, irrespective of the near-term decisions of customers. The business pays these employees until the lack of customers makes it evident to the employer that he has misjudged customer demand. Only then will he fire some or all of his employees.

The wage is a signal to other workers and other employers regarding the prevailing conditions of supply and demand. If this wage is a market-clearing wage, there will be no rival workers offering to work for a lower wage for the same job, and there will be no rival employers offering to pay more.

3. Stone

A union organizer comes before workers and makes this argument. "You are being exploited by your employer. He is able to exploit you because you are just one person. Your employer is rich. He does not have to worry about feeding his family. You are not rich. You are living paycheck to paycheck. You are in a weak position as a solitary employee. But if you gather together with other employees, you can challenge this exploitation. You can bargain collectively. Your employer cannot afford to fire all of you at once. You will then get paid what you are really worth."

This may sound plausible. The workers individually do not have any clout. The employer can fire any individual. He can replace the fired individual. The replacement is willing to accept the job. This seems unfair.

Why is it unfair? Two people come to an agreement: the employer and the replacement worker. The replacement worker has a right to bid. Workers compete against workers. Employers compete against employers. Why is this immoral? Why is this unfair? But the union organizer says that it is unfair.

If the government does not interfere, the union organizer can test his theory of wage formation in the marketplace. He can persuade workers to threaten to quit. Maybe the employer will cave in. Or maybe not. He may decide to replace all of the strikers. This is what Ronald Reagan did in 1981 when the Air Traffic Controllers union (PATCO) went on strike. He gave them a deadline. If they refused to return to work, he said he would replace all of them. Most of them refused. He replaced all of them on that day. No planes crashed. The union had overplayed its hand. Members thought Reagan was bluffing. They were wrong. No other government union ever tried this again.

The simpler the job, and the more numerous the number of unemployed workers who can do this job, the easier it is for the employer to break the strike.

Union organizers know this. So do union members. So, unions pressure the government to force employers to negotiate "in good faith" with union members if half of the workers, plus one person, vote to be represented by the union. This be-

gan in 1935 in the Untied States. The government passed the
Wagner Act. It set up the National Labor Relations Board to
enforce the new rules. The government threatened any employer with violence—fines—if he did not allow the union to
recruit members. If they won the election, it became illegal for
the employer to replace striking workers.

Thus, unions that gain a 50% plus one vote operate in a judicial system in which there are government-enforced price
floors on wages. Non-union members may bid for jobs, but
it is illegal for employers to accept these bids. They must join
the union. They must pay union dues. They may not be paid a
wage below that which the union, through government coercion, has imposed on the employer.

4. Costs

Price floors create gluts. When the new wage rates are imposed by the government through union negotiation, these
wages attract potential workers. The union cannot allow them
into the union. There would be too many members for the
business to employ at the above-market wages secured by government coercion. In short, supply and demand are thwarted,
but not at zero cost.

These workers are surplus workers at the above-market
wages. The labor markets do not clear at these above-market
wages. There is greater supply of labor than demand for labor
at the above-market prices.

The workers who cannot get into the union cannot get access to these high-paying jobs. So, they must look elsewhere
for employment. Who will hire them? The answer is clear:
employers whose employees have not yet voted 50% plus one
vote to be represented by a union. So, now there are extra unemployed workers to employ. If the competing employer had
been allowed to offer jobs to these workers, they would have
gotten jobs. They would be available to hire only at a wage
higher than the competitor's. But these workers cannot get
these plum jobs. So, they compete against each other for jobs

at the non-unionized business. This employer now has an ideal situation. He can offer lower wages to these unemployed workers. They have no known alternatives. If they had better offers, they would accept them.

So, the result of higher wages paid by employers who pay above-market wages is lower wages for non-union members in non-union businesses. Wages are higher for union members, but they are lower for non-union members.

What if the unions organize these non-union members? They will be able to get higher wages if they get 50% plus one vote. Then the newly unionized company will not be able to hire as many workers at the higher price. The same process will repeat until the unions have no more companies that can afford higher wages. Then marginal companies will start going bankrupt. There will be more workers seeking jobs.

Unemployment will rise among the ranks of workers who are the victims of union membership discrimination. Wages will fall in the non-unionized sectors. The success of some union members to obtain higher wages will be paid for by the failure of non-union members to obtain employment at the previous low wage of the industry. Wages will fall.

The non-union companies will now offer lower prices to customers. They can hire cheaper workers. Either their profits increase (higher profit margins) or else their market share does (lower prices). These firms increase at the expense of unionized firms.

Customers who would have profited from the productivity of unemployed workers will not benefit.

The government may pass laws to support unemployed workers. Taxpayers will fund these expenditures.

5. Consequences

In nations in which the government supports union policies, the result has been widespread unemployment among those groups that have been blocked by unions from becoming members. In some nations, younger workers have suffered huge rates of unemployment—rates approaching 50%. In other nations, racial groups have had higher unemployment.

Employers have been unable to fire workers and replace them. This has led to reduced labor output and lower customer satisfaction.

Inside a nation, some local jurisdictions have laws prohibiting union shops, meaning businesses that are closed to non-members. In the United States, these "right to work" states attract businesses that want freedom of contract. Some established businesses move to these states. In other cases, older businesses remain in states that do allow union shops, but new business formation is higher in the "right to work" states. Higher business profit margins exist in these states. In the United States, the auto industry has shifted from Michigan to the Southeast as a result of these local laws.

Union restrictions on access to jobs have also led to offshoring: businesses set up plants in nations without strong unions. The firms then import the goods that are produced by their branches located overseas.

Imports from abroad increase. Foreign manufacturers are able to produce goods by paying workers less than what unionized firms can pay. They sell these goods at prices below those offered by unionized firms. This leads to calls by unions to restrict imports, thereby reducing customer choice.

As populations become more educated, workers move into management and clerical positions that are not unionized. Manufacturing moves offshore. Union membership as a percentage of the labor force declines. In the United States, union membership peaked in 1953 at about 35%. It has fallen to about 10% as imports have increased and education levels have risen.

Conclusions

Unions have the ability to increase wages only when the government forces businesses to bargain with them collectively. Union members benefit from high wages, but these higher wages are paid for by workers who cannot get into the successful unions, and who must then seek employment on worse terms than were available prior to the success of the unions in extracting above-market wages for their members. This effect on employment benefits employers whose companies have not been unionized. The state's coercion of certain employers acts as a subsidy to non-unionized companies. Wages fall in these companies.

Thus, as a result of economic analysis, we can say for certain that unions raise wages only when the state enforces collective bargaining. Wage rates in some companies are higher as a result, but wages in most companies are lower as a direct consequence of the government's wage floors, which are enforced selectively.

Sadly, Hazlitt refused to affirm this from start to finish in this chapter. *This is by far the worst chapter in Hazlitt's book.* He refused to make this the central principle of this chapter: *union wage rates as one more example of government-imposed price floors.* He began the chapter with this:

> The power of labor unions to raise wages over the long run and for the whole working population has been enormously exaggerated. This exaggeration is mainly the result of failure to recognize that wages are basically determined by labor productivity.

The power of unions to raise rates has not been merely exaggerated; it does not exist at all without government coercion. Unions cannot possibly raise wages in general. Their ability to do this in any economic sector is based exclusively on government coercion: price floors. All price floors have the same result: gluts of the protected commodity, which means unemployed resources. He should have begun with an analysis of union wage rates as government-imposed price floors. He should have ended with this.

It gets worse.

All this does not mean that unions can serve no useful or legitimate function. The central function they can serve is to assure that all of their members get the true market value of their services.

How? Are unions the source of accurate information on wage rates throughout the economy? What is the evidence for this? Do they inform workers of higher wages in other industries? In round numbers, never. The greatest social and legal arrangement for the transmission of accurate information in man's history is the free market's price system. Unions are no more to be trusted to inform their members of accurate pricing of wages than government-created cartels of producers are to be trusted to inform their members of accurate pricing of commodities. Both the union and the cartel are the creations of government restrictions on entry.

It gets worse. It gets much worse.

But in recent years, as their power has grown, and as much misdirected public sympathy has led to a tolerance or endorsement of antisocial practices, unions have gone beyond their legitimate goals. It was a gain, not only to health and welfare, but even in the long run to production, to reduce a seventy-hour week to a sixty-hour week. It was a gain to health and leisure to reduce a sixty-hour week to a forty-eight hour week. It was a gain to leisure, but not necessarily to production and income, to reduce a forty-eight-hour week to a forty-four-hour week.

Unions had exactly zero to do with these gains, if we are to believe Hazlitt's economic analysis. The thesis of this chapter is that wages are raised—i.e., hours are reduced, but at the same pay—only by investment.

Thus we are driven to the conclusion that unions,

though they may for a time be able to secure an increase in money wages for their members, partly at the
expense of employers and more at the expense of non-
unionized workers, *do not, in the long run and for the
whole body of workers, increase real wages at all.*

If we believe Hazlitt's analysis of productivity and wages,
and also his arguments on the cartel nature of unions, there
is no evidence that unions raise wages for the whole body of
workers in the short run, either.

The belief that they do so rests on a series of delusions.
One of these is the fallacy of *post hoc, ergo propter hoc,*
which sees the enormous rise in wages in the last half
century, due principally to the growth of capital investment and to scientific and technological advance, and
ascribes it to the unions because the unions were also
growing during this period.

Conclusion: only through increases of labor productivity
can wages rise. This raises the central analytical issue: unions
have had nothing to do with increased investment and technological innovation. This leads us to a conclusion: *unions
have had nothing to do with increased labor productivity.*
Therefore, they have not raised wages in general for workers.
They have raised wages for their members only in businesses
that have been unionized. They have achieved this only at the
expense of lower wages for nonunion workers, who are forced
to accept jobs that they would not have accepted, had the government not made competitive bids from rival workers illegal
for businesses to accept.

Hazlitt began the chapter with an assertion of the fixed relationship between rising wages and rising labor productivity, but he failed to defend this line of reasoning from start to
finish. If he had, he would never have referred to any earlier
"legitimate function" of labor unions in reducing labor hours

and making more healthy workplaces.

So, Hazlitt's statement about the "legitimate function" of unions is nonsensical, assuming that his discussion of labor productivity and wages is correct. I assure you, it is correct.

Conclusion: Hazlitt was squishy on unions.

Further Reading

For supporting material, go to bit.ly/CEIOL-Doc-19.

−20−

"Enough to Buy
Back the Product"

It is naught, it is naught, saith the buyer: but when he is gone his way, then he boasteth (Proverbs 20:14).

Once again, Hazlitt returned to the issue of government price fixing. In Chapters 13, 15, 16, 18, and 19, price fixing was in the form of price floors. It is in this chapter, too.

In this variation on the same theme—price floors—Hazlitt invoked a slogan which is rarely heard any longer: "Workers must be able to buy back their product." It was never widely heard. He said that there were two sources of this slogan: Marxists and labor union leaders. Today, Marxism is dead, and most labor unions are, too. So, we no longer hear the argument.

Hazlitt did not say what the defenders of this idea proposed as a solution. Is the government supposed to raise the wages of workers by decree? All workers? Just some workers? By what percentage? The promoters of this idea never said what they meant. This is one reason why the slogan never caught on.

Hazlitt argued that this argument was a variant of the just price doctrine of the medieval world. Wages had to be just, the theologians said, meaning ethically righteous, meaning fair. But what is fair? The serious theologians of the Middle Ages, including Thomas Aquinas, recognized this problem, and they generally argued that market prices are just, most of the time.

Orthodox Marxist theorists never argued for economic justice. Marx argued that all morality is simply window dressing

183

for class economic interests. The orthodox Marxists did not think that any tinkering with market prices by the state could solve the inherent economic problems of capitalism; only proletarian revolution would. They never talked about how prices would be set in the world beyond the proletarian revolution. Neither did Marx.

This left labor union spokesmen as the promoters of this idea. The best statement of this idea was made by Walter Reuther, the head of the United Auto Workers Union. He also was the head of the Congress of Industrial Organizations (CIO), the more militant of the two major American labor unions, the other being the AFL: American Federation of Labor. Reuther said this years after Hazlitt wrote the book. At a meeting at the Ford Motor Company in 1954, this exchange supposedly took place. It was published in 1955.

> CIO President Walter Reuther was being shown through the Ford Motor plant in Cleveland recently.

> A company official proudly pointed to some new automatically controlled machines and asked Reuther: "How are you going to collect union dues from these guys?"

> Reuther replied: "How are you going to get them to buy Fords?"

Reuther cited variants of this exchange in subsequent speeches. The original is close enough for economic analysis. We hear the same arguments today with respect to robotics and computerization. But no one today thinks the problem can be solved by hiking wages by law. The fear today is future massive unemployment at any wage level.

The analytical error of Reuther's comment comes from this fundamental idea: *capitalist employers are exploiting workers by using machines to replace them.* We have heard this warning for several centuries.

Machines do not buy anything. Workers buy things. The economic question is this: "Are workers paid the value of their contribution to the production process?" If not, why not? More to the point, if not, how not? In a competitive market, how is it that one employer can exploit workers by not paying them what they are worth? Why don't rival employers "raid" the exploiter's operation by offering higher wages?

This takes us back to the issue raised by Hazlitt in so many chapters: "How are prices formed in a free market?" Then there is this follow-up question: "If the state interferes with this price-setting process, what will be the results?"

As always, I begin with the question of ownership, which is a legal issue that has economic ramifications. The reason why I repeat the following two sections is this: the error that Hazlitt was dealing with is the same one as before, namely, a government-mandated price floor.

1. Owners

One set of owners possess money: business owners. They may also possess capital equipment, which includes land and buildings. They possess business plans. These plans involve hiring human laborers.

Another set of owners possess the ability to deliver labor services. These people are eligible to rent out these services.

A third set of owners will decide at some point whether to purchase goods and services that have been produced by a combination of business capital and labor services. They will determine retroactively which sellers prosper and which do not.

All participants possess the legal right to bid.

2. Window

The window is a product of a society's moral, legal, and cultural traditions and institutions. This window is known as the free market. Those with money to spend (buyers of goods) work out arrangements with people who want to sell goods to buyers (buyers of money).

In this system, people who hire workers seek to locate people who rent out these services at some price. Economic exchange always depends on an agreed-upon price. Buyers compete against buyers. Sellers compete against sellers. Only in the final stage of the hiring process does face-to-face bargaining take place: would-be employer vs. would-be employee. The prospective employer does not know how little money the prospective employee will accept, and the prospective employee does not know how much money the prospective employer will pay. In this zone of ignorance, there may be negotiating. But probably not. Time is not a free resource. Employers usually make this offer: "Take it or leave it. I am too busy to negotiate."

The employer acts as an economic agent of future customers. He will give them an opportunity to buy the output of his production process. The employer also acts as an economic agent of his employees. In order to earn money, employees must sell their services to customers. The employees do not know how to market their services directly to customers, but the employer believes that he does. So confident is the employer that he is willing to pay money to the employees to perform certain tasks, irrespective of the near-term decisions of customers. The business pays these employees until the lack of customers makes it evident to the employer that he has misjudged customer demand. Only then will he fire some or all of his employees.

The wage is a signal to other workers and other employers regarding the prevailing conditions of supply and demand. If this wage is a market-clearing wage, there will be no rival workers offering to work for a lower wage for the same job, and there will be no rival employers offering to pay more.

3. Stone

Hazlitt did not describe the stone. He argued that critics also never described it.

How are we to know, however, precisely when labor does have "enough to buy back the product"? Or when it has more than enough? How are we to determine just what the right sum is? As the champions of the doctrine do not seem to have made any clear effort to answer such questions, we are obliged to try to find the answers for ourselves.

He argued that the idea of a lack of purchasing power by workers is a variation of what he called the "purchasing power argument." Capitalism supposedly withholds from workers the full value of their production. This was Marx's argument, although Hazlitt did not identify it here: the argument regarding surplus value. Hazlitt zeroed in on the error.

In an exchange economy everybody's income is somebody else's cost. Every increase in hourly wages, unless or until compensated by an equal increase in hourly productivity, is an increase in costs of production.

This stone is another variant of every intervention by the state to secure wages that are higher than what are produced by the free market's system of supply and demand.

4. Costs

Hazlitt returned to his familiar critique of government price fixing.

This brings us to the general meaning and effect of economic equilibrium. Equilibrium wages and prices are the wages and prices that equalize supply and demand. If, either through government or private coercion, an attempt is made to lift prices above their equilibrium level, demand is reduced and therefore production is reduced. If an attempt is made to push prices below their equilibrium level, the consequent reduction or wiping out of profits will mean a falling off of supply or new production. Therefore an attempt to force prices either above or below their equilibrium levels (which are the levels toward which a free market constantly tends to bring them) will act to reduce the volume of employment and production below what it would otherwise have been.

This is the standard argument against price controls in all systems of free market economics. He referred to *equilibrium* prices. Equilibrium is a concept of physics. He meant *market-clearing*. Everyone who wants to buy at this price can do so, and everyone who wants to sell at this price can do so. There is neither excess demand nor excess supply. *Only one price will produce this result.*

Therefore, any attempt by politicians or bureaucrats to set a price higher or lower will produce excess. A price floor will produce excess supply over demand. The high official price lures sellers and drives away buyers. A price ceiling will produce excess demand over supply. The low official price lures buyers and drives away sellers.

If the state sets wages higher than the free market would produce, there will be unemployed laborers. Why? Because the law drives up production costs. Businesses fire workers who do not provide sufficient output to justify keeping them on the payroll. This is another version of a minimum wage law. In this case, however, it may not apply to all jobs. It may apply only to some jobs. The promoters of the slogan never said.

Hazlitt also added a discussion of monetary inflation. If the central bank creates fiat money, the price level will rise. Then there may not be unemployment. The artificially high wages will then not purchase as many goods as before. This means that real wages have fallen. Although he did not say this, his discussion meant this: if real wages fall, then we are back to square one. The market has established a market-clearing price. So, the critics will complain again. Labor is still not able to buy back its output.

5. Consequences

The consequences of this idea were minimal. Almost no one ever understood it. It did not affect government economic policy in the form that we read it here. The critics were never clear on how high specific wages should be forced up by law.

If you do a Web search for the phrase, "buy back the product," and also search for "wages," you will find that most of the hits are links to this chapter of Hazlitt's book. In retrospect, he did more to give life to this slogan than any labor union leader, and surely more than any Marxist.

Conclusions

This is the most jumbled chapter in the book. Hazlitt gave lots of unconnected examples. They are difficult to follow. An example:

> The belief that the price increase would be substantially less than that rests on two main fallacies. The first is that of looking only at the direct labor costs of a particular firm or industry and assuming these to represent all the labor costs involved. But this is the elementary error of mistaking a part for the whole. Each "industry" represents not only just one section of the productive process considered "horizontally," but just one section of that process considered "vertically."

> Thus the direct labor cost of making automobiles in the automobile factories themselves may be less than a third, say, of the total costs; and this may lead the incautious to conclude that a 30 percent increase in wages would lead to only a 10 percent increase, or less, in automobile prices.

This is not clear.

He neglected to go for the jugular. He did not offer this response:

> In a free market economy, workers are paid enough to buy their production. Through competitive bidding—employers vs. employers, workers vs. workers—each factor of production is paid what most people think it is worth. There may be an error, but it will be corrected when an entrepreneur exploits this error by buying low in order to sell high. A worker who participates in any production process will be paid the full value of his unique contribution to total output. If he is not, then another employer will lure him away with a higher wage.

This is the traditional response of free market economists to this ancient analytical error. The critics of capitalism ignore the competitive bidding process, where suppliers of labor compete against each other, and buyers of labor compete against each other. Out of this objective price competition come specific wages for specific workers. Hazlitt here avoided the analytical question: "How are wages set?"

He identified one economic cost to society. If the government imposes additional costs of production by raising legal wages, the result will be reduced production. The wealth of society will decline, even though members of a specific government-favored group's income will increase. He repeated this argument in his chapters dealing with price controls, either price floors or price ceilings. It is a correct argument.

It is an incomplete argument. The major social cost is not higher unemployment. *The major social cost is the violation of property rights.* If the government makes it illegal to make and accept bids, then it undermines private ownership. How? *By undermining disownership.* A bid to buy is a bid to sell—to disown. If you have no right to disown, then you are not a full owner.

Here is the problem with his line of reasoning. He resorted to full employment to challenge the legitimacy of this argument. He does this in every chapter on government price fixing. This weakened the entire book. In this chapter, he was explicit in a way that he was not in earlier chapters. He rested his case for the "best" outcome on economic output alone. This is a moral judgment. He sneaked it though the back door. He stated this clearly in this chapter. In the next-to-the-last paragraph, he wrote this:

> As to the prices, wages, and profits that should determine the distribution of that product, the best prices are not the highest prices, but the prices that encourage the largest volume of production and the largest volume of sales. The best wage rates for labor are not the highest wage rates, but the wage rates that permit full production, full employment, and the largest sustained payrolls. The best profits, from the standpoint not only of industry but of labor, are not the lowest profits, but the profits that encourage most people to become employers or to provide more employment than before.

My approach is fundamentally different. I do not begin with maximum economic output as an ideal. Why not? Because economic output is a result. I begin with judicial theology: the question of what is morally right. Economists should begin with ownership, not output. They should define "best" in terms of ethics and law, not economic output. They should start with private ownership: its obligations, its moral foundations, and its consequences.

Economic analysis should begin with this issue: *the legal system's criteria for linking human action with legal responsibility.* Then it should trace the results of this legal order as they apply the principle of ownership/disownership in a world governed by scarcity.

The free market economy produces the highest rate of production, full employment, and the largest sustained payrolls because of the private ownership of property. The free market's pricing system, which is the outcome of competitive bidding, is in turn the outcome of the biblical judicial principle of ownership/disownership. The profit-and-loss system of economic sanctions is why the free market produces the best outcomes, as Hazlitt defined them.

Hazlitt did not start with the legal system. Few economists do. But I do. He did not start with ownership. Few economists do. But I do.

Further Reading

For supporting material, go to bit.ly/CEIOL-Doc-20.

21

The Function of Profits

After a long time the lord of those servants cometh, and reckoneth with them. And so he that had received five talents came and brought other five talents, saying, Lord, thou deliveredst unto me five talents: behold, I have gained beside them five talents more. His lord said unto him, Well done, thou good and faithful servant: thou hast been faithful over a few things, I will make thee ruler over many things: enter thou into the joy of thy lord (Matthew 25:19–21).

This passage appears in the most famous passage of the New Testament that deals with the final judgment. It is a parable about an owner who entrusts coins to three servants. The servants are stewards. Then he leaves. When he returns, he demands an accounting. Two servants produced a profit. The third buried his coin. The master has no gain on his investment. The master condemns the man.

This was one of Jesus' pocketbook parables. He knew that his listeners were interested in money. He knew they would understand the parable. The message was clear: a steward is an economic agent of the owner. The owner expects a positive rate of return on assets transferred to the steward. In short, he expects a profit on his investments. Breaking even is not good enough. It is clear how he would have regarded a loss.

The language of business is obvious. There is capital. The owner hands over these capital assets to subordinates. He diversifies his portfolio: three men, each with skills. He is future-oriented. He does not know how these stewards will perform. He has a plan: to judge their ability to perform profitably. When he returns, he demands an accounting. The two stewards who produced a profit gain a reward: additional capital. They will remain stewards of the owner. One steward failed to make a profit. He is fired—permanently.

There is no hint that profits are evil. There is more than a hint that losses are to be avoided. If breaking even gets you fired, think of what the consequences are for losses.

Why would Jesus use this as a parable of the final judgment? Because the final judgment is the archetype—the ultimate model—for all accounting. We are held responsible for our actions. We possess property, but only as stewards of God. Our ownership is a form of trusteeship.

Why would anyone imagine that profits are illegitimate? Yet millions of people do. Hazlitt dealt with this hostility in this chapter. He attributed this hostility to ignorance about the function of profits in a free society. This chapter is more explanatory than an example of a specific intervention by the state. In this sense, it is like Chapter 15: "How the Price System Works."

1. Owners

If an individual owns a small business, he is responsible for its operations. It must produce a stream of profits if he is to remain in business. What is true of a sole proprietor is equally true of a large corporation. In this case, the owners are shareholders. They delegate to managers the responsibility of producing a profit. The managers are stewards, not owners.

Other owners are potential customers, who own money, which is the most marketable commodity.

2. Window

The window is the legal structure that identifies who is responsible to whom. The senior managers in a corporation are responsible to shareholders. They must report to shareholders. The shareholders have the legal authority to replace senior managers. If they are not sufficiently organized to do this, they may sell their shares. This will tend to lower the price of the shares. This sends a signal to other investors: the company's management is failing to produce profits. A new owner, sometimes called a take-over specialist, can then buy shares cheaper than before. If he buys a sufficient number of shares, he can fire existing managers. He may head up a group of outside investors who buy shares. Their goal is to fire managers, re-structure the company, and make a profit. Then the price of the shares will presumably rise. They bought the shares low. They can now sell the shares high.

How do they make a profit? By selling to customers at prices that cover costs and also provide a profit. If there were no profit potential, they would not have bought the shares. If they had not bought the shares, they would not have been in a position to replace the existing managers. In that case, existing managers would have continued to make mistakes. Potential customers would not have become actual customers. Profits would have proven elusive.

In this system of ownership and disownership, the hope of profit drives managers and owners. To make profits, managers must serve customers. The customers possess money. Their decisions to buy or not to buy determine retroactively which producers were successful with their plans. What is the proof of their success? Profit. The profit system delivers planning and production into the hands of entrepreneurs, but the success of their plans depends on customers. Customers "hold the hammer." Their retroactive control over the production process depends on the profit-and-loss accounting system.

This system is future-oriented. It is based on an inescapable fact: no one knows the future perfectly. No one knows what customers will want in the future—in what quantity, at what price, and in what location. This includes customers. Customers expect businessmen to guess what customers will want in the future, and then plan for this.

The free market's rule is this: sellers compete against sellers; buyers compete against buyers. With respect to competition among sellers, Hazlitt wrote this:

> The function of profits, finally, is to put constant and unremitting pressure on the head of every competitive business to introduce further economies and efficiencies, no matter to what stage these may already have been brought. In good times he does this to increase his profits further; in normal times he does it to keep ahead of his competitors; in bad times he may have to do it to survive at all. For profits may not only go to zero; they may quickly turn into losses; and a man will put forth greater efforts to save himself from ruin than he will merely to improve his position.

The stewards have four-way responsibility: upward to the owner, outward to customers, downward to any employees, and inward to themselves—their goals, dreams, and standards.

3. Stone

Hazlitt was not clear about the nature of the stone. One possibility: government price fixing.

> One of the greatest dangers to production today comes from government price-fixing policies. Not only do these policies put one item after another out of production by leaving no incentive to make it, but their long-run effect is to prevent a balance of production in accordance with the actual demands of consumers.

Another possibility: a profit ceiling.

> But if profits are limited to a maximum of, say, 10 percent or some similar figure, while the risk of losing one's entire capital still exists, what is likely to be the

effect on the profit incentive, and hence on employment and production? The wartime excess-profits tax has already shown us what such a limit can do, even for a short period, in undermining efficiency.

Could this be an excess profits tax? These were imposed in World War II. He offered no other examples. He could have. Business taxes of any kind restrict profits. Government regulations reduce profits. But these laws are not passed in the name of limiting profits. On the whole, American voters have been unconcerned politically about high business profits. They have not pressured Congress to pass laws with a specific goal of limiting profits.

4. Costs

The main cost of the broken window is a reduction of customer authority. The business owner and the senior managers must pay attention to state bureaucrats, who have the power to impose losses. The degree of authority possessed by customers is reduced. Profit and loss now depend increasingly on meeting standards set by bureaucrats. In the name of protecting consumers, bureaucrats reduce the authority of bureaucrats by reducing the customers' ability to reward successful businesses. Hazlitt wrote:

> One function of profits, in brief, is to guide and channel the factors of production so as to apportion the relative output of thousands of different commodities in accordance with demand. No bureaucrat, no matter how brilliant, can solve this problem arbitrarily. Free prices and free profits will maximize production and relieve shortages quicker than any other system. Arbitrarily fixed prices and arbitrarily limited profits can only prolong shortages and reduce production and employment.

This interference by the state reduces the flow of information from customers to business decision-makers. This flow of information is based on prices and accounting. The decision-makers need this information to guide production in order to meet future customer demand. The state's interference with profits is like tossing mud balls onto the windshield of a racecar in the middle of a race.

5. Consequences

With the exception of government-regulated public utilities, which are protected from competition, and which are guaranteed a fixed rate of return by the regulatory agencies, there is no systematic American political program of profit-reduction in the name of limiting profits to protect the public. This is advantageous for customers.

Conclusions

Profits are ethically legitimate. Jesus taught this. Hazlitt did not mention this. Profits are necessary for society. Jesus implied this. Hazlitt was explicit. Someone must guide production. Who should this be? Someone will consume production. On what legal basis? Every society must answer these questions:

1. Who is in charge? In a free society, these: owners.
2. Who serves as economic agents of the owner? In a free society, these: entrepreneurs.
3. What are the rules? In a free society, these: "Make profits, not losses."
4. What are the sanctions? In a free society, these: profits and losses.
5. Which organizations inherit? In a free society, these: profitable ones.

Profits and losses are the sanctions in a free market social order. Without these, producers are flying blind. Without these, customers lose control over who wins and who loses. Any attempt by the state to reduce profits will increases losses. This interference will have two negative effects: (1) blurred vision for producers; (2) reduced control by customers. The winners will be politicians and bureaucrats who enjoy exercising power.

Further Reading

For supporting material, go to bit.ly/CEIOL-Doc-21.

22

The Mirage of Inflation

Thy silver is become dross, thy wine mixed with water (Isaiah 1:22).

T he prophet Isaiah was publicly criticizing the nation as a whole. He also spelled out the crimes of political rulers. They were bribe-takers. They were companions of thieves (v. 23). They rendered false judgment, cheating widows and orphans (v. 24). But before these crimes, he mentioned monetary debasement: cheap metals mixed in with silver. The word "debase" comes from "base" metals—cheap metals. This was monetary inflation.

Isaiah was making a point. The sins of the nation had debased the nation. The corrupt practice of silver smelters was to mix low-cost metals into the molten silver. This produced bars that looked like pure silver, but were not. This was counterfeit metal. It was deceptive. People in Israel initially thought that the silver bars had high value because of silver's scarcity, so the smelters continued to deceive the public. More counterfeit silver bars had come into circulation than there would otherwise have been, had smelters not debased the bars.

Isaiah did not say that prices had risen. But his listeners knew. And it was not just the smelters who were doing this. The wine makers were, too. There was larceny in their hearts.

He warned of a coming judgment by God. He used the language of smelting.

Therefore saith the Lord, the LORD of hosts, the

mighty One of Israel, Ah, I will ease me of mine adver-
saries, and avenge me of mine enemies: And I will turn
my hand upon thee, and purely purge away thy dross,
and take away all thy tin: And I will restore thy judges
as at the first, and thy counsellers as at the beginning:
afterward thou shalt be called, The city of righteous-
ness, the faithful city (vv. 24-26).

The society was ethically corrupt. The society was ethically
counterfeit. But the purging would be real.

The debasement of Isaiah's day was kids' stuff compared to
today. That was because of the limits of deception. Pour too
much dross into the molten metal, and it will no longer look
like silver. The modern world has debased its coinage. No nation's mint issues silver coins as common coinage—only as
collectibles. By the mid-1960's, silver coins were replaced by
counterfeits.

In 1965, most money was not coinage, as is true today. Most
money was a combination of paper currency and bank checks.
Printed currency of any denomination all looked alike. The
"dross" was paper and ink, worth a few cents. The "silver" was
the face value of the bill. The central bank's profit—mark-up—
on printing these bills was enormous. The governments had
laws against printing counterfeit bills, but their central banks
printed nothing but counterfeit bills. What held this process
in check was the threat that people could bring in their paper
money or write checks and get gold coins. That ended in Europe in late 1914: World War I. It ended in the United States
in 1933. It ended for silver coins in the United States in 1964.
(Note: in the summer of 1963, I converted almost all of my
money into silver coins, which I got at a bank at face value. By
the end of the summer, these coins started going out of circulation as a result of Gresham's famous law: "Bad money drives
good money out of circulation.")

Today, most money is digital. All digital money is counterfeit money. We do not even see the money any longer. We use

pieces of plastic. Computers communicate with each other.

Counterfeit money is morally wrong. It is a form of theft. But economists do not like to invoke ethics in their analysis of economic cause and effect. They also do not like to criticize theft by civil governments as theft, for that brings up this ethical issue: "Thou shalt not steal" (Exodus 20:15). It does not say, "Thou shalt not steal, except by majority vote."

Hazlitt followed the lead of Ludwig von Mises. He used the word "inflation" to refer to fiat money creation. He did not use it to describe the *result* of fiat money creation: rising prices. Isaiah preceded both of them in this regard. He identified the evil of inflating—and it *is* evil. Mises did not mention ethics and economics together. Neither did Hazlitt. Murray Rothbard did. He always labeled inflating as theft.

1. Owners

The best definition of money, analytically speaking, is this: *the most marketable commodity.* Throughout history, this has meant gold and silver. Before the sixth century, B.C., in Asia Minor this meant bars. After, it meant coins.

There are owners of non-monetary assets. There are owners of monetary assets. Why does anyone hold money? Because money is used to make purchases. It is a medium of exchange. It is owned only because the owners expect others to exchange non-monetary assets for money. Money has a wide market. It has an instant market. You don't have to argue with a seller to accept your money at the retail price for whatever he is selling. You don't need to take a discount for cash. You may even get a discount for cash.

2. Window

When we are talking about a scarce resource, more is better . . . at the same price or lower. If an individual gains more, he is better off. This is also true of groups. When there is more to be had because the supply has risen, this is good for everyone.

With respect to money, more is also better, but only for individuals. When people inside a monetary union all gain more money because the supply has risen, they are not better off. This makes money unique. When one person gives another person some money, the recipient is better off than before. The person giving money may be better off, too. "It is more blessed to give than to receive" (Acts 20:35). But he is worse off monetarily. If the central bank were to create new money, and then give it away by crediting everyone's bank account with more money, this would not make society richer.

Why the difference? Because money is desirable in exchange, but not for personal consumption. In *Robinson Crusoe*, Crusoe is on the half-sunken empty ship that carried him to the island. He loads up with all of the ship's supplies that he can carry. He then comes across the captain's money box. He takes some coins, but only after he has loaded up a raft full of useful tools. The coins will be valuable if a ship ever comes and rescues him, but not otherwise. If he is not taken back into society, the coins are useless except as decorations.

Think of a counterfeiter. He prints new money. He spends it on items he wants. He is better off after these trades. So is the person with the fake money, as long as he never figures out that it is fake, and as long as no one else finds out. But society is not better off. It is worse off. A counterfeiter is on the loose.

The government does not worry about a lone counterfeiter. It worries about imitators. One counterfeiter who spends money only on lunches and car repairs is not a threat. But he must be prosecuted as a warning to potential rivals.

The counterfeiter's biggest rival is the national government's central bank. Actually, the counterfeiter is copying the central bank. The central bankers resent this as an invasion of the bank's turf. They call on the government to track this criminal down and arrest him. In the United States, the agency in charge of tracking down counterfeiters is the Secret Service, which also defends the life of the President.

If an inventor makes a health-improving discovery, and he puts it into the creative commons on the Internet for free, lots of people will soon be better off. In contrast, if a counterfeiter finds a way to produce untraceable counterfeit bills on a cheap 3-D printer, and then he releases this information on the Internet, society will soon be worse off. People will steadily lose faith in the currency. This will reduce its purchasing power, i.e., raise prices. This undermines the value of all currency bills, which are valued only for expected future exchanges. So, if the supply of a resource increases, its price will fall. This is an advantage to consumers. In contrast, if the money supply increases, its value will fall. This is a disadvantage to consumers. They cannot easily find a replacement currency that other people will sell goods in order to obtain.

If the future value of money is widely expected to be about the same as the past value of money, this maintains the value of money. Any unexpected increase in the money supply upsets people's expectations about the future value of money. The cost of holding money therefore increases because of this increased risk: holding depreciating money.

3. Stone

The stone is thrown by a government-licensed bank or bank cartel that has the authority to create money out of nothing—these days, by computer entry. This process is initiated by the nation's central bank. It can also be done by a commercial bank that operates under the authority of the central bank. Because the government licenses and protects the banking system from bank runs, the banks create money. They lend it into circulation, and charge interest to the borrowers. It is profitable to counterfeit money.

Central banks prior to 2008 usually bought only debt certificates (IOU's) issued by major governments. Since 2008, there is evidence that some central banks also buy stocks or stock-related assets. They surely buy the debts once held by banks that are facing bankruptcy.

The banks purchase IOU's. The borrowers then spend this money to buy whatever it is that they buy. Those sellers who receive this money then deposit it in their banks. This spreads digital money through society.

This new money does not create wealth. It redistributes wealth. Those sellers who get access early to the newly created legal counterfeit money go out and buy things at yesterday's prices. The new demand from the new money has not yet registered on sellers of goods and services. So, with more money to spend, these newcomers with their freshly created counterfeit money start buying. This takes goods and services off the market. Other potential buyers cannot locate these goods and services, because someone else got there first.

We know that a free market economy is a giant auction. The auction has one rule: *high bid wins*. What if you went to an auction to bid on items. You notice that there is a man in the back of the room with buckets full of paper money. He keeps talking with people in the back of the room. They sign a piece of paper, and the man with the buckets hands over a bucket. You notice that the bids of the people in the back of the room are higher than the bids of people at the front of the room.

The auctioneer is delighted. You are not delighted. You cannot compete with the people in the back of the room. You are going to go home with the same amount of money, but no bargain items. Next week, you will have made a deal in advance with the guy with the buckets full of money. You will sign the pieces of paper—IOU's—in order to get your hands on a bucket of money.

Others will do the same. Pretty soon, the prices at the auction are higher than they were two months ago. There are no more items to buy, but prices are higher.

The winners are the people who started going into debt at the first auction, when prices were lower. They took home the wealth at bargain prices. There has been no creation of new wealth. There has only been a redistribution of existing wealth.

4. Costs

The auction model works for considering costs. First, the people who did not figure out how the new system works are losers. They would have taken home more goods from the auction, had the man with the buckets of money not shown up.

Second, everyone who attends the auction has greater debt. Everyone had to sign a series of IOU's in order to get a continuing supply of newly created counterfeit money.

Third, prices are higher.

Fourth, if the supply of counterfeit money stops, everyone who took on added debt will be in trouble. Prices at the auction will not go higher, but the bidders will find that they must now bid lower for items. Why? Because part of their ordinary income must now be used to pay off the pile of debts. They cannot go to the auction with as much money as they used to.

Fifth, prices at the auction now revert back to where they were before the man with the buckets of money showed up. This means that the bidders who paid high prices at recent auctions find that the value of these items is falling. They looked like good deals when the bids at the auction were rising, but now the bids are falling. So, bidders will bid less at the next auction. They are burdened with debt, and now prices are falling. They will fear to bid high prices.

Here, we can see what happens to an economy that is manipulated by central banks and commercial banks. When the banking system started creating fiat (legal counterfeit) money, the new money created the illusion of new wealth. Those who spent their newly created money early won. This was the boom phase of the economy. But now the economy is in the bust phase: a recession. Demand has fallen. Debt has risen. Consumers reduce their spending. The auctioneers of the world now find that demand is lower. Their profits are lower. But they had expanded in the boom phase. They borrowed money to hold more auctions.

A real auction deals with used goods. In the overall economy, the auction is for all goods. The boom persuades businesses to borrow, buy raw materials, rent buildings, and increase production. Then, without warning, demand falls. These businesses are now unprofitable. Their markets are shrinking. Buyers are holding back. Now businesses start going bankrupt. The auctioneer arrives to pick up inventory. This new supply leads to lower prices at the auction. The recession may turn into a depression. It did in the decade 1930–1939, all over the world.

The price signals during the boom phase misled investors, producers, and consumers. These people made mistakes. They took on too much debt. Now the day of reckoning—the day of accounting—has arrived. Profits turn into losses.

How does Bastiat's analysis apply here? What is the thing not seen? This: the array of prices that, apart from legalized counterfeiting, would have been produced by the auction's rule of high bid wins. We see the booming auction and mini-auctions all around us. We do not see the world that would have prevailed without legalized counterfeiting. As Hazlitt put it, inflation produces a mirage. Thirsty people, lost in a desert, walk toward the mirage: a hoped-for oasis of life. It is not there. It is an illusion. At some point, the thirsty wanderers will realize this. But they will be far from an oasis. They will be far deeper into the desert than they would have been, had the banking system not produced a seemingly endless series of mirages.

5. Consequences

When the West went off the gold coin standard late in 1914, as a result of the early phase of wartime financing, the depositors lost their gold. They had been promised for a century that if they deposited gold coins at a bank, they would be paid interest, and they could get their coins back at a fixed price. That was a massive deception. Then, late in 1914, the central banks and governments of Europe reneged on the promise. They stole the gold. Then they issued fiat money. Except for Great Britain, 1925–1931, no European nation ever again restored a gold coin standard. President Roosevelt in the spring of 1933 did the same thing. He was even worse. Not only would the banks not honor their promises to redeem (sell back) gold at $20 an ounce, he declared it illegal for Americans to own gold. He declared this on his own authority. Congress later passed a law validating Roosevelt's unilateral declaration.

From 1934 until August 15, 1971, central banks and governments could buy gold from the United States at $35 an ounce. Following Roosevelt's precedent, President Nixon on a Sunday evening unilaterally announced that the United States would no longer honor its pledge to redeem gold to foreign central banks and governments. He "closed the gold window," just as a handful of economists, including me, had for several years predicted he would. The Federal Reserve began creating fiat money on a massive scale to get the nation out of a recession. The result was rising prices. Prices rose from 1971 to 1981 at a more rapid rate than at any time in the history of the United States in peacetime. There were a series of recessions: 1975, 1980, 1981–82. From 1971 until 2016, consumer prices rose by almost six-fold.

All over the world, central banks followed the lead of the United States. They inflated. The result was rising prices in every nation. Debt also rose: government, corporate, and personal. A level of debt now exists that has not existed since 1946, when Hazlitt wrote his book. That debt was abnormal: the product of World War II. Today's debt levels have become normal. Politicians, corporate CEO's, and households are used to these debts. But if central banks cease inflating, these debts will be revealed as unsustainable. At that point, there will be debt liquidation and bankruptcies. Central bankers fear this, and so they return to inflating. This continues the bad investing that prevailed in the previous boom phases.

Conclusions

In 1972, a collection of articles by F. A. Hayek was published in Great Britain: *A Tiger by the Tail*. It was on central bank inflation. The tiger today is much larger. It is much more dangerous. The world is still on the tiger's back.

Money is the most marketable commodity. It is the central economic institution. It is the result of the division of labor, and it has become central to the division of labor. It is the source of price signals. The price system is the greatest source of information in history. But central banks and commercial banks now manipulate this price signal system by their policies of legalized counterfeiting. They have done so aggressively ever since late 1914 in Europe and ever since 1933 and then 1971 in the United States. They have placed the world on a fearful tiger. That tiger is fed by fiat money. It gets ever more ravenous.

The greatest threat economically today is a debt implosion. The level of worldwide debt is greater than ever before. It is unprecedented. It can only be sustained by new rounds of monetary inflation.

The previous periods of monetary inflation, all over the world, have extended the division of labor. The price signals have been manipulated by the banking industry. These signals are as counterfeit as the money. If the banking system ever ceases to inflate, bankruptcies will multiply. Today's division of labor has been artificially extended by false price signals. We are in an international auction that is dependent on new rounds of fiat money, with the men in the back of the room lending out buckets of digital money.

We call a mild contraction of the division of labor a recession. A major contraction is called a depression. The world has not seen a depression since 1940. People are not mentally, emotionally, or financially prepared for another depression. This is why central banks continue to inflate. But the end of this policy is hyperinflation. That, too, contracts the division of labor.

When the division of labor contracts, most people get poorer.

Further Reading

For supporting material, go to bit.ly/CEIOL-Doc-22.

−23−

The Assault on Saving

The LORD shall open unto thee his good treasure, the heaven to give the rain unto thy land in his season, and to bless all the work of thine hand: and thou shalt lend unto many nations, and thou shalt not borrow (Deuteronomy 28:12).

He shall lend to thee, and thou shalt not lend to him: he shall be the head, and thou shalt be the tail (Deuteronomy 28:44).

There are two passages in the Bible that present the fundamental principles of economic growth: Leviticus 26 and Deuteronomy 28. They are parallel passages. They present a series of sanctions. The sanctions are mainly economic. About one-quarter are positive sanctions. Three-quarters are negative. They are covenant sanctions. They have to do with obedience and disobedience to God's laws. Hence, they are both judicial and ethical. They make it clear that *economic theory must be seen in terms of ethics.* They teach that economic theory cannot be ethically neutral. Good economic results are the product of good economic behavior.

These two verses contrast the two systems of sanctions. The first appears in the section on positive sanctions. It promises success through lending. Lending is part of a program of wealth accumulation. It begins with agriculture. Good crops depend on rain. But this is only one aspect of national wealth. The net productivity will affect the whole range of economic endeavors. This includes money lending. The sign of economic success is the capital required to become a lender. Such capital is a mark of a successful person who is following a successful program. So, when it comes to success, being a creditor is a worthy goal. Avoiding debt is also a worthy goal.

In contrast is the second sanction. It is the reverse of the positive sanction. In this case, the cursed man is the debtor. But he is not the foreigner. The foreigner is in a position of authority. The mark of success is to be the head. The mark of failure is to be the tail. Half a millennium later, Solomon wrote: "The rich ruleth over the poor, and the borrower is servant to the lender" (Proverbs 22:7).

Because of the myth of economic neutrality, we find that most economists today praise both debt and credit. Are they not both legitimate economic ends? Are they both not goals of human action? Are they not different aspects of the same voluntary transaction? Therefore, are they not marks of a free society? They are marks of a free society, but they are not equal. He who lends is extending the influence of his worldview. He who borrows is subordinating himself to the creditor's worldview. While both lending and borrowing should be legal, he who pursues consumer debt is clearly a fool. This places him in the category of a covenant-breaker. He places himself in the category of "losers in history": functionally subordinate to another man's god.

This outlook is at war with modern economics. Modern economics is officially neutral methodologically. The Bible is not. The Bible praises thrift and curses debt. It makes it clear that thrift is a moral good. Debt is evidence of a moral weakness: a concern with present consumption at the expense of economic independence.

This is not a criticism of debt that finances a program of capital accumulation, such as investing in real estate. But it warns the entrepreneur that such a debt-funded business venture is risky. The person who collateralizes his capital may lose it. A businessman may take a loan, but if the bank refuses to renew it, he may lose his business. He is the servant to the lender.

So, the Bible makes it clear: it is a moral obligation to lend. This is an affirmation of a program of saving. Why? Because of the biblical concept of redemption. To redeem means to buy back. Christianity preaches that Jesus Christ came to redeem His people. How? By living a perfect life, and then dying as a substitutionary payment to God: His death for His people's otherwise mandatory eternal death. But this was preliminary to comprehensive redemption: buying back a fallen world for His people. His people will inherit the earth. This is stated repeatedly in the Psalms. "His soul shall dwell at ease; and his seed shall inherit the earth" (Psalms 25:13). But the means of this program of redemption is through service, not military conquest. Jesus said:

> But Jesus called them unto him, and said, Ye know that the princes of the Gentiles exercise dominion over them, and they that are great exercise authority upon them. But it shall not be so among you: but whosoever will be great among you, let him be your minister; And whosoever will be chief among you, let him be your servant (Matthew 20:25–27).

Lending money to people who want to buy consumer goods is part of this program of redemption. *Lending brings present-oriented consumers under the influence of future-oriented lenders.* This means that one of the goals of lending—a form of thrift—is to permanently consume less that you save. Saving is part of a program of cultural dominion. It is to extend the kingdom of God by means of a lifetime of thrift, including money-lending. This means that thrift is not only for future consumption. It is for future dominion.

Adam Smith wrote this: "Consumption is the sole end and purpose of all production; and the interest of the producer ought to be attended to only so far as it may be necessary for promoting that of the consumer. The maxim is so perfectly self-evident that it would be absurd to attempt to prove it." The goal of production is indeed consumption, but not for the producer. For the Christian, production should be seen as God's mandated means to a series of mandated ends. One of these ends is capital accumulation, not for the purpose of consumption, but for dominion. The very rich understand this. A multimillionaire or a billionaire does not sacrifice his life to make another million dollars in order to spend it on more consumption. He does it to extend his influence.

It is the supreme economic mark of covenantal rebellion in both modern economic theory and policy that government debt is praised as an aspect of wise fiscal policy. Only slightly less perverse is the suggestion that consumer debt is positive because it stimulates production. This is what is known as *demand-side economics*. It is the essence of Keynesianism. Keynes recommended government deficits as a way to produce national wealth.

At the beginning of chapter 16 of Keynes' *General Theory of Employment, Interest, and Money* (1936), Keynes wrote what has become a legendary critique of saving. He argued as follows: because saving is no guarantee of future consumption, the act of saving reduces present employment. It reduces present demand for goods, and therefore it hampers the economy. If this were a general principle, then it would mean that, throughout history, saving has been a liability, and it has retarded economic growth.

> An act of individual saving means—so to speak—a decision not to have dinner to-day. But it does *not* necessitate a decision to have dinner or to buy a pair of boots a week hence or a year hence or to consume any specified thing at any specified date. Thus it depresses the business of preparing to-day's dinner without stimulating the business of making ready for some future act of consumption is not a substitution of future consumption-demand for present consumption-de-

mand,—it is a net diminution of such demand. . . . If
saving consisted not merely in abstaining from present
consumption but in placing simultaneously a specified
order for future consumption, the effect might indeed
be different. For in that case the expectation of some
future yield from investment would be improved, and
the resources released from preparing for present consumption could be turned over to preparing for the future consumption (pp. 210–11).

While Hazlitt did not quote this passage explicitly, his chapter was written to counter the policy implications of this passage. This passage, perhaps more than any other passage in
Keynes' work, is the foundation of the fundamental errors of
Keynesianism in general. It is Keynes' intense hostility to saving, and his call for government expenditures in a time of economic depression to offset the employment-destroying effects
of saving, that are the heart of the Keynesian system.

1. Owners

One owner is the owner of money. He can spend it on consumption. He can also spend it on a tool of production. He can
lend it to someone who also can either buy consumer goods or
buy tools. The owner even has the right to hoard his money.

A second owner is the owner of a credit score high enough
to enable him to secure a loan. His credit rating is a form of
personal capital. The higher his rating, the greater the value of
his personal capital. But this capital can be used to obtain a consumer loan (higher interest) or a producer loan (lower interest).

Then there are the owners of raw materials, tools, land, consumer goods, and labor services. They want to sell these various forms of property.

2. Window

The window is all of the capital markets and all of the consumer goods markets. These markets serve buyers and sellers.

Someone with money can spend it in any of these markets. There are sellers who are happy to make a sale, at least at retail prices. These sellers compete for the money that money owners have to spend.

Sellers of consumption goods make their case: "Enjoy what I have to sell. You deserve it. You've worked hard for your money. You only go around once in life. You can't take it with you." Sellers of capital make their case: "Save for a rainy day. You never know what will happen next. Look to the future. You want a comfortable retirement. Think about college for your kids." Sellers of charitable programs make their case: "You can save a life. You can change the world. You can feel better about yourself. Wealth has its responsibilities."

Nobody says this: "Go to the bank and withdraw currency. Hide it in a safe place." In any case, someone with $10,000 or more can't do this without violating some law or drawing attention to himself.

The person who has money in the bank is lending it. The bank has invested those digital currency units. The money is not idle. Someone will be receiving money. This money will be used to buy things. These purchases keep the economy running smoothly. People with money change their budgets from time to time, but all of the money available to them is being put to what owners regard as productive uses.

If he transfers his digital money to a seller of goods or services, the recipient will put the money to use. How? By either keeping it in his bank or by spending it on whatever he needs to keep his operation running.

If the person withdraws currency and hides it, this will have no measurable effect. No one will notice. Anyway, he hopes so. Even if millions of bank depositors did this, consumers would benefit. Sellers would have to lower their prices. Sellers do not like this, but consumers do. When you go to an auction to buy something, you want to see a sparse crowd. The auctioneer will be unhappy, but you will not be.

3. Stone

Keynes' discussion of saving as a cause of reduced consumption and therefore economic stagnation ignored Bastiat's analysis. Keynes failed to consider the uses to which saved money would be put in the private sector. The money might be loaned or invested in businesses that organized resources for future output. This would increase future consumption. But it would also be used for present consumption. Employees hired by these firms would receive wages. The other use for invested money was lending to consumers, who would use this money to buy goods and services. Thus, Keynes' concern about saving as a source of reduced demand was an error. Analytically, it is the central error of Keynesianism. Yet it is rarely mentioned, even by critics of Keynesianism. This reveals the extent to which mainstream economics rests on a complete misunderstanding of economic cause and effect. From 1936 until the present, Keynesian economists have had a free ride. But free rides, like free lunches, are mythical. Someone pays for them.

Politicians are pressured during a recession to spend money on various projects. There are relief projects: free money for unemployed workers, or low-interest loans for businesses. The latter payments are not regarded as relief, but they are. They involve getting something for nothing.

Keynesian economists constantly cry out for more government spending. The government has the ability to "get the economy rolling again," the politicians are told. So are the voters. The solution to the recession is government spending on anything. Keynes used this example.

> If the Treasury were to fill old bottles with banknotes, bury them at suitable depths in disused coalmines which are then filled up to the surface with town rubbish, and leave it to private enterprise on well-tried principles of laissez-faire to dig the notes up again

(the right to do so being obtained, of course, by tendering for leases of the note-bearing territory), there need be no more unemployment and, with the help of the repercussions, the real income of the community, and its capital wealth also, would probably become a good deal greater than it actually is. It would, indeed, be more sensible to build houses and the like; but if there are political and practical difficulties in the way of this, the above would be better than nothing (*General Theory*, p. 129).

First, it costs money to fill the bottles. Second, someone must be hired to hide the bottles in the mine. Third, someone must be hired to dig up the bottles. Fourth, someone would spend the money. For efficiency's sake, modern governments skip the bottles and the money. They just spend the money on what President Obama said were "shovel-ready projects." He was wrong. Few jobs were created by this welfare program. But the money was spent.

But the money would have been spent anyway. If the central bank created the money out of nothing by purchasing Treasury debt, the money would have been spent. Anyway, this would have been the case prior to December 2008. When the Federal Reserve began offering a tiny amount of interest on excess reserves (0.5% per annum), commercial banks have sent lots of their deposit money to the Federal Reserve, which then to spend it by purchasing Treasury debt. This kept the Federal Reserve's policies of hyperinflation of the monetary base from $900 billion to $4.2 trillion in six years from becoming money. Consumer prices barely rose.

4. Costs

There is the general cost: the disrupting effects of the state's entering the capital markets. The politicians want to spend the money on projects they think will gain a net increase in votes at the next election. So, they can raises taxes, borrow money, or have the central bank print it. In a recession, politicians are afraid to raise taxes. So, they usually resort to borrowing and monetary inflation.

If they borrow from investors, this shifts money out of those investment categories that the investors previously preferred. The money goes into spending categories that politicians prefer. So, there will be a different set of beneficiaries. This process transfers money out of the private sector and into the coffers of the government. Then the money gets spent.

These costs are associated with the reduction of productivity that results from the re-allocated money. If government bureaucrats spend the money, those groups that receive the money are benefited. Those groups that do not get the money are harmed. But members of these groups do not "follow the money." They do not perceive that the beneficiaries of a government spending program benefit at the expense of members of groups that would have sold something to the original investors, who instead turned their money over to the Treasury.

Investors who turn over the use of their money to businesses that produce for future customers are providing the means of future consumption. They trust the judgment of the business managers who make the decisions about the goods and services that future consumers will be willing and able to to pay for. These business managers are specialists in making these estimates. They are under the restraints of accounting: profit or loss. Their success rests on their accurate forecasting and appropriate strategies of production.

Other investors turn over their money to the government, which will be used to buy votes. The politicians will battle politically over the budget. The outcome of these battles will determine which of the favored groups get access to the money.

The government will spend all of it. Then future politicians will decide what to do to repay investors: (1) raise taxes, (2) borrow more money, (3) sell IOU's to the central bank, which will create the money out of nothing.

Government spending of borrowed money reduces economic growth. That is to say, it reduces the supply of future goods and services.

Private spending of borrowed money may increase economic growth if it is borrowed by businesses that sell to consumers. Or it may be borrowed by consumers, who then spend it. If they buy consumer goods, the money goes to sellers who specialize in production. Some of the profits they make will be re-invested in the seller's business, or used in the name of the business to benefit investors.

When a civil government increases its percentage of the nation's borrowed money, this reduces the rate of economic growth. It also increases the government's debt. In terms of Keynes' original theory, the government will pay off part of this debt in boom times, and increase debt in recessions. In operation, the debt almost always rises. The only school of economic opinion that opposes the increase of government debt, and which advises the repayment of borrowed money through constant budget surpluses, is the Austrian School. In the history of the United States, the government has been debt-free in only one fiscal year: 1835.

5. Consequences

By redirecting their capital from output-increasing enterprises to governments, investors have lowered economic growth. This has reduced the wealth of every Western nation. Median household income in the United States stagnated after 1973, after 25 years of high growth. Economists debate over the causes of this slowdown. Non-Keynesian economists would look carefully at the evidence of the increase in government debt as a factor.

Most national governments increase their debt every year. Most of them have debts owed to investors in the range of 100% of the nation's annual production. Some are three times national production.

This attitude toward debt has trickled down to the citizens.

They are also heavily indebted. But because they must make monthly payments on their debt, the percent of their after-tax income that goes for debt servicing is quite constant. In the United States, household debt servicing varies from about 15% of after-tax income to 18%. Corporate debt has also increased. The combined debts of the national government, regional governments, businesses, and households sometimes reach four to five times the total income of a nation.

When combined with the unfunded liabilities of government-funded retirement programs and government-funded programs of health care for the aged, the level of national government debt is many times the official figure. Some estimates of the present value of the unfunded liabilities of the United States government for these two programs are in the range of $200 trillion. Compared to the official debt of about $19 trillion (2016), the official debt is minimal. There will be a default at some point. As to which kinds of debt and which creditors are sacrificed, we can only guess. But default is inevitable. This will have negative political, social, and economic consequences.

Conclusions

Keynesian economics reinforced politicians' spending preferences in raising the level of government debt after 1945. Hazlitt recognized this shift in opinion years before he wrote *Economics in One Lesson*.

Increased debt has made economies more vulnerable to recessions. Debt obligations remain in good times and bad times. When governments, businesses, and households use the rising income during boom times to increase their debts, the bust times create financial hardships. There is a debt ratchet phenomenon all over the world. The threat of bankruptcies in the next recession has increased. This is called debt de-leveraging. People who have budgeted for income in their retirement will be startled to learn that bankruptcies of pension plans will cut into their expected income.

More important than this is a shift of attitude toward debt. The willingness to sacrifice present consumption for the sake of investing is the mark of a future-oriented person. This is a good way to define "upper class." These people value the future more than their middle-class and lower-class peers do. We have seen a shift over the last two generations in the direction of lower-class attitudes.

Consumers have concluded that it is easier to succumb to the lure of present consumption than to remain debt-free. This is the loser's mentality, according to Deuteronomy 28:44. Christians should avoid this mentality. It rests on bad theology.

Further Reading

For supporting material, go to bit.ly/CEIOL-Doc-23.

−24−

The Lesson Restated

Thou shalt not steal (Exodus 20:15).

Hazlitt's version of the lesson was different from mine. What was the lesson, according to Hazlitt, that he was trying to make? Here is his first paragraph of Chapter 24:

> Economics, as we have now seen again and again, is a science of recognizing secondary consequences. It is also a science of seeing general consequences. It is the science of tracing the effects of some proposed or existing policy not only on some special interest in the short run, but on the general interest in the long run.

The trouble with this summary is this: most members of scientific guilds claim exactly the same thing that Hazlitt claimed for his version of economics. They claim to follow the implications of the science's truths. They claim to look at the overall picture, which they call the general view, which is supposedly based on general laws. They also claim to deal adequately with specific cases. So, what is it that distinguishes economic science from political science or educational science or psychology or sociology or physics?

I gained a different lesson from Hazlitt's book: *Follow the money . . . backwards.*

This phrase, "follow the money," came into the American vernacular because of the movie, *All the President's Men* (1976). This was a movie on President Nixon's forced resigna-

222

tion in 1974, which came because of two diligent reporters for *The Washington Post*, Woodward and Bernstein. This three-word phrase was the recommendation given to the reporters by an anonymous tipster whom they called "Deep Throat." (That was in turn a reference to a famous pornographic movie of the era.) What is not widely understood is this: the two reporters do not remember their source ever saying this. The phrase does not appear in their book. The screenwriter, William Goldman, is probably the source.

I regard my four-word phrase as the essence of Bastiat's general analytical principle: the broken window. What he told us in 1850 was simple: follow the money . . . backwards. Every time somebody recommends that the government intervene in order to protect an industry, or a special group, and the advocate does this in the name of helping the general public, we can be sure that the person making the recommendation has not followed the money backwards. Anyway, he has not told the general public the truth, the whole truth, and nothing but the truth. He may persuade the public, and he may also persuade politicians, that the state should intervene to help this group in the name of helping the general public. But if an economist follows the money backwards, he will find that the claim regarding the benefits for the general public is false. The only reason why the promoter successfully makes this claim is because the public refuses to follow the money backwards.

If you follow the money backwards, you will find out that there were benefits associated with that money before the window was broken. The promoter who wants the government to intervene wants the voters to *follow the money forward* to all the benefits the money will produce. The money will stimulate the economy, he says. But if we follow the money backwards to the person who owned it prior to the envy-driven action of the person who threw a stone through the window, we will find that there were other things that the window's owner preferred to do with the money.

In chapter 23, "The Assault on Saving," we discover a more fundamental truth than might have been the case in 1850. The money was already being used for productive purposes. Today, an individual has the money in a bank. The bank is providing services for this deposit. The bank is also lending the money to a borrower. The money is being used for one set of purposes, and these purposes are highest on the list of the person who owns the money. So, when the stone goes through the window, and the owner calls the window repair shop, he will have to pay for this by taking money out of the bank. This is bad for the person who owned the window. This is bad for the local bank that took in his deposit. This is bad for anybody who expects to get a loan from that bank.

We can easily follow the money forward. That is the analytical problem. But it takes considerable skill and insight to follow the money backwards. There is no question that of all economists in history, Bastiat was the first to see it, and Hazlitt was the most successful in applying it.

At this point, I am trying to do my fair share of promoting the concept.

The most important economist in history who refused to follow the money backwards was John Maynard Keynes. The 20th century after 1936 was increasingly constructed on the intellectual foundation laid by Keynes in *The General Theory*. The heart of his analysis was chapter 16, which is the main source in modern times of the assault on saving. Keynes made the mistake that Hazlitt's book is devoted to avoiding: he refused to follow the money backwards. He said that the saver is a liability to the economy, because the money he saves will not be used for consumption.

Keynes was not the first person to make this mistake. Even before him, an economic crackpot known as Major Douglas built a peculiar economic cult that was based on exactly this idea. It was called Social Credit. Keynes recognized the importance of Douglas' contribution, and he actually praised Douglas in *The General Theory* (pp. 371–372). I have written a book refuting Social Credit, and I am the only person who has: *Salvation Through Inflation*. I wrote this about 75 years after Douglas wrote his first book. Modern economists ignore him, for good reason, but Keynes did not ignore him. Keynes dressed up Douglas' position with jargon and equations. But, analytically speaking, Keynes' position was Douglas' position.

Here is the problem we face. The entire economics profession has ignored the principle discussed in Hazlitt's book. There are non-Keynesian economists, but none of the economics textbooks goes after Keynes on the obvious point, namely, that the money that the saver supposedly would have wasted on thrift would in fact have increased employment. The textbooks also do not point out the related error, namely, that all the money collected by the government from investors who would otherwise have invested in the private sector is taken out of the private sector. The government does not get this money from heaven. It may get the money from the central bank, but then we have the problems associated with fiat money creation, which is simply legalized counterfeiting.

The critics of Keynes never call central bankers legalized counterfeiters. There is no textbook used in any college or high school that says this. Yet this is the economics of central banking and all fractional reserve commercial banking.

The textbooks do not hammer away at the fundamental error of Keynes regarding thrift. Even Hazlitt did not mention Keynes by name in Chapter 23. In 1959, he wrote an excellent refutation of Keynesianism, *The Failure of the "New Economics,"* but almost nobody has read it.

Here is my conclusion: *there is something more involved here than simply economic ignorance.* Hazlitt convinced no certified economist by means of Chapter 23. He convinced almost nobody with his book in 1959. He also published a collection of essays by economists who were critical of Keynes, *Critics of Keynesian Economics* (1960). No one in academia paid any attention to that book, either.

Hazlitt was correct in identifying the fallacy of the broken window as a consummate example of the unwillingness of economists to follow the implications of the science of economics. He was a clear writer. He usually got to the point pretty fast. Yet with respect to the entire economics profession, he had zero influence outside of the Austrian School of economics.

By now, you can see the logic of the broken window fallacy. Why has it not also occurred to the entire economics profession? There is something deeper here than simply economic ignorance. There is something deeper than the absence of high IQ's. Professional economists are intelligent people. The best of them probably are geniuses. Yet this simple concept, first proposed in 1850, was ignored systematically from 1850 until 1946. Then, after 1946, the economics profession systematically ignored Hazlitt's applications of the fallacy of the broken window.

I contend that this is not a matter of ignorance. It is not a matter of people's unwillingness to study economics. What we have here is blindness. It is willful blindness. It is self-conscious blindness. It is an unwillingness to take a simple analytical principle and then follow it to its conclusions.

My conclusion is this: at bottom, the unwillingness of economists to understand this rests on ethical rebellion. It is not a matter of ignorance. It is a matter of ethics. It rests on a violation of the fundamental principle: "Thou shalt not steal."

The modern welfare state, the modern redistributionist state, the modern Keynesian state, the modern socialist state, and the modern communist state, all have this in common: *they are based on theft*. From top to bottom, from start to finish, they are all based on theft. They are based on this principle: "Thou shalt not steal, except by majority vote."

Because there is larceny in the hearts of people, they want to believe that fiat money can deliver them out of their position of debt. They will pay off their creditors with depreciated money. They also want to believe that their refusal to plan for their retirement should not be held against them. The public should be taxed, so that they will receive retirement money. The same thing is true of their views regarding socialized medicine and its variations around the world. They want to get their hands in other people's wallets, and they will not tolerate a prophet coming before them and saying, "You are all thieves." In Isaiah's day, they did not listen to Isaiah, who warned them: "Thy silver is become dross, thy wine mixed with water." They did not care.

Keynesian economists are court economists. Keynes gained his career's major triumph only when he presented a convoluted defense of existing interventionist, theft-based policies of Western governments to deal with the Great Depression. Only when he became an apologist for national theft on a massive scale did he change the minds of a younger generation of economists.

Keynes was an apologist for theft by the ballot box. The politicians loved his message, and so did a generation of younger economists, who wanted to see the state expanded, and who wanted to see their influence increase by giving advice to politicians and bureaucrats. They saw the tremendous personal leverage that they could gain by invoking the state as an agency of scientific wealth redistribution, but without becoming targets of the criticism that they were socialists or communists.

In other words, I do not think this is primarily an intellectual problem. I think this is primarily a moral problem. This is why I have written this book. I want Christians to understand what is at stake here. This is a war, not simply for the minds of men, but for the souls of men. Economists do not talk this way. They may understand the war for the minds of men, but they categorically reject the idea that they are in any way involved in a struggle for the souls of men. They want economic science to be neutral. Yet the triumph of Keynesianism indicates that economics is not neutral. It rests on the appeal of a particular form of morality. This morality is simple to state: "Thou shalt not steal, except by majority vote."

There is obviously a political problem when special interests appeal to the power of the state to redistribute wealth in their direction. They do not want this discussed in terms of theft, but it really is theft. But there is a much greater problem. The public does not perceive such appeals as organized forms of theft. The voters do not resist. They also want to get their hands into their neighbors' wallets. They are also ready to form a special interest political group to get their hands into their neighbors' wallets.

Then there is the economic problem of motivation. Any special-interest group that is seeking a major redistribution of wealth is intensely interested in persuading politicians of either the validity of their position or at least the political advantages associated with their position. They are highly focused, because there is so much money at stake. In contrast, the public does not pay any attention. The public, which will pay its fair share, meaning its unfair share, of the loot extracted from them, have other concerns. There are so many special-interest groups trying to get into their wallets, that they never focus on stopping a particular group. It is just too much trouble. The payoff is too low. But the payoff is enormously high for the special-interest group. The likelihood of success is so low for any political opposition that political opposition never forms.

My conclusion is based on the principle of following the money. In a cost-benefit analysis, it does not pay the opponents to fight the special-interest group. It is cheaper to organize their own special-interest groups, and try to get their hands on some of the loot.

Hazlitt tried to maintain ethical neutrality in economic analysis. He never described any of the special-interest groups as a form of organized crime. He did not discuss wealth redistribution in terms of systematic theft. When he attempted to refute these policies, he failed to gain academic supporters. He should have known from the beginning that this would be the case. Economics would have told him as much. The special-interest groups have so much to gain. In contrast, opponents of any specific program of wealth redistribution will not be able to gain enough political support to stop the particular special-interest group from getting what it wants. Economically speaking, Hazlitt should have concluded that the book was an exercise in futility. Economics should have told him that the book would not be successful in rolling back the modern Keynesian welfare state.

I do not expect my book to have any affect in slowing down the expansion of the Keynesian welfare state. My goal is longer term. I want to explain to Christians why, after the collapse of the Keynesian state has taken place, this disaster took place.

Because of Keynes' hostility to saving, and because of Keynesianism's lackadaisical attitude toward the expansion of government debt, there is going to be a Great Default. *All Western governments are going to default on their welfare state programs.* Economically speaking, meaning actuarially speaking, all these old age programs are bankrupt. They will all go belly-up.

There will be enormous pain after this happens. I do not regard myself as some modern Isaiah. Besides, I know what happened to Isaiah. Nobody paid any attention to him. The judgment came, but that was over a century later. But, in retrospect, the message of Isaiah has come down through the millennia. It did not penetrate the thinking of his contemporaries, but it left a cogent record for the rest of us.

I don't think the Keynesian welfare state can be reformed. I think that at some point it can be replaced. But this replacement must be made in terms of ethics, not the broken window fallacy. It does no good to try to roll back any of the 23 variations of the broken window fallacy that appear in this book and in Hazlitt's book. That is because the issue is not primarily intellectual. The issue is primarily ethical.

People cannot follow long trains of reasoning. This certainly applies to economic reasoning. We see this in the case of Hazlitt's book. He was not able to convince any Keynesians to follow the money backwards. They did not rethink Keynesian economics in terms of this fundamental error, which lies at the heart of all Keynesianism. If professional economists refuse to follow the money backwards, and they deny the obvious implications of government debt in undermining the private sector, then why should we expect the average person who might read this book, meaning you, to be able to formulate systematic arguments against any of these policies? Why should I expect you to be able to organize a special-interest group to fight 100 or 200 or 500 or 5,000 special interest-group programs?

After the Great Default, there is going to be a time of reconsideration. People are going to want to know why it happened to them. At that point, perhaps some of the arguments in this little book will penetrate the thinking of a few Christian leaders. But until the pastors are willing to go to the verses that I have exegeted, and then present this exegesis to their congregations, I do not expect a major change. Until these issues are presented in terms of theology, ethics, and justice, I do not think my criticisms of these policies will have any greater effect than Hazlitt's criticisms did.

His book is still in print 70 years after he wrote it. Because of the Web, and because of Kindle, I hope that my book will also stay in print. It doesn't even have to stay in print; it just has to stay on a computer screen. Anybody can press the "print" icon. Staying in print is easy. Attracting readers is not. Motivating readers is not.

What I am saying is this: *This is a battle for the souls of men.* This is not simply a series of intellectual debates within a particular academic discipline. The modern world rests, economically speaking, on bad ethics. It rests on this principle: "Thou shalt not steal, except by majority vote."

Ideas have consequences. Even more important, behavior has consequences. In Leviticus 26 and Deuteronomy 28, we see that there are economic consequences, good and bad, in terms of the society's adherence to fundamental ethical law. Until people believe this, I do not think it is going to do a great deal of good to follow the money backwards. It is a valuable intellectual exercise, but it is not going to change most people's behavior, especially in the voting booth.

Further Reading

For supporting material, go to bit.ly/CEIOL-Doc-24.

Conclusion

Hazlitt's conclusion, Chapter 24, restated his thesis: the conceptual necessity of following the money in order to consider what an individual would have done with his money, had the state not intervened to "break his window."

It did not ask that most crucial of questions, "What is to be done?" Lenin asked it in 1902, parroting an earlier revolutionary, Cherneshevsky, who had asked this four decades earlier.

In 1946, there was not much to be done. When Hazlitt finished his manuscript on March 25, the season had just turned spring. Given the topic of his book, it was economic spring as never before in America's history.

The United States was the economic colossus of the world. Never before in history had one nation attained this degree of economic supremacy. Canada and the United States were almost a single trading zone. They had emerged from World War II physically unscathed.

The managerial transformation caused by the war had not been foreseen in 1941. It had restructured American manufacturing. The mass production techniques of the wartime industries would soon go into full gear to meet demand from the consumer economy.

There was another huge advantage, one unforeseen by most analysts. The mass inflation of the Federal Reserve during World War II had been suppressed by price and wage ceilings. The government adopted rationing as the means of allocation. By the end of the year, most of these ceilings were repealed. Prices adjusted upward. In doing so, the price and wage floors of the 1930's ceased to have any influence. Prices after 1946 were above the old floors. Production adjusted to the new demand. The depression did not reappear, because the conditions that had caused it—price floors—no longer functioned.

Meanwhile, the world's economy was in tatters. Western Europe was rubble. Japan was, too. England was close to bankruptcy, a shell of its former financial self. It would soon surrender its empire, which it could no longer afford to police. India and Pakistan gained their independence in 1947. Hong Kong was not yet the powerhouse it was to become. The same was true of South Korea. China was poor, and in 1949 it fell to the Communists, and it soon became much poorer. The Soviet Union was an economic basket case, and it would remain a basket case until it went out of existence in December 1991. It had military power, but nothing else.

The United States could export to any society that had dollars. New lending arrangements, private and federal, began to make available American production to foreign borrowers. America's banks had money to lend, and the Western world was ready to borrow on terms favorable to the American banking system.

This was a new world order. The Great Depression did not return. The recovery was produced by the freeing up of the economy. Most price and wage controls ended the following October. Set free after five years of price and wage ceilings, which followed a decade of price and wage floors, the economy boomed. But from that time on, bright young Keynesians and aging academic defectors took full credit for the recovery. They explained the boom in terms of massive federal wartime debt, which had been funded heavily by Federal Reserve inflation. The Keynesians soon replaced the aging professors, who had come of age before the Great Depression, and who had generally remained mute throughout it. In 1948, Paul Samuelson's *Economics* textbook announced the coming of this new world order. It became the dominant textbook in higher education for the next three decades.

The Bretton Woods agreement of 1944 went into operation in 1946. This gold exchange standard substituted the dollar for gold. It was a license to print money without suffering a gold run on the Federal Reserve. Hazlitt saw through this bureaucratic substitute for the pre-World War I gold coin standard, and he said so in print. That cost him his job at *The New York Times*.

When Hazlitt sent his page proofs off to the printer, Leonard E. Read was ready to open the tiny, underfunded Foundation for Economic Education in Irvington-on-Hudson, New York. FEE would become the lone voice for Hazlitt's brand of economics over the next two decades. FEE did not have a monthly magazine for another decade, when it began publishing *The Freeman*.

Ludwig von Mises had not yet written *Human Action*, which appeared in 1949. There were only a few newsletters in 1946 that promoted the free market, and their combined subscriber bases were in the low four-figures. The main one was *Human Events*, which did not focus on economics.

There were three tiny publishing houses: Regnery, Devin-Adair, and Caxton. They did not have mailing lists. They did not have access to bookstores. Their marketing was based on word of mouth.

What was to be done? Keep on writing for the handful of people who might read.

That was then. This is now.

The Keynesian era has led to exactly what anti-Keynesians predicted in Hazlitt's day: massive debt, public and private. This debt cannot be repaid. It was never intended to be repaid by those who issued it. Keynesianism is an economic philosophy based on the idea of ever-growing national government debt, and ever-growing central bank inflation to secure below-market interest rates for this debt. Today, short-term federal debt is essentially free of charge for the government: a fraction of a percent. It has been so ever since 2009.

This too shall pass.

Keynes had predicted this in *The General Theory* in 1936: capital costs of zero (pp. 220–21). That seemed to be the nuttiest prediction in his book, but here we are: the marginal efficiency of capital—government capital—is zero. So is the rate of interest for T-bills. Yet this has created a crisis for Keynesian theory: the fearful "zero bound." Central bank monetary inflation can no longer lure entrepreneurs to borrow, even at zero. The Federal Reserve gets little or no bang for its bucks. Then what can it do if the economy falls into another recession comparable to 2008–9? What happens to central bank anti-recession policy when the only policy in its tool kit is the only one it has ever had: monetary inflation? It is pushing on a string.

In the next recession, there will be a scramble for liquidity. Lenders will search for a government-guaranteed return of capital. They will sacrifice the return on capital. They are doing this with T-bills now. The quest for guaranteed returns will become a mania. In 2016, all Swiss government bonds had negative interest rates. German bonds were negative except for 30-year bonds. This was also true of Japanese government bonds.

What will happen to entrepreneurship then? What happens to Keynesian capitalism? What happens to economic growth when the federal government absorbs the bulk of the available capital of the nation?

What Is to Be Done?

I ask the Keynesians: What is to be done?

The deficit of the U.S. government in fiscal 2015 was above $400 billion. This was in the sixth year of an economic recovery. In a recession it will more than double. What is to be done?

The present value of the unfunded liabilities of Social Security and Medicare is now in the range of $200 trillion. What is to be done?

The Keynesian prescription of federal deficits and monetary debasement is barely sustaining the American economy.

Western Europe, Japan, and China have adopted the same prescription. They are all struggling.

What is to be done?

Keynesians are the ones with the blueprints. They are the ones who proclaim the efficacy of central planning through federal deficits and central bank inflation. They are the ones who exercise faith in grand designs.

Defenders of the free market do not offer blueprints that will get us from here to there. They do not trust in central planning. They have faith in the general blueprint: private ownership, monetary voluntarism, the abolition of central banking, low taxes, the abolition of government guarantees, free trade, freedom of entry into banking, and the reduction of the federal deficit to zero, as it was in 1835 for one magnificent fiscal year.

What is to be done? Bide our time. We do not need a grand plan to shrink the federal government. The Keynesians are laying the foundations for the Great Default—all over the world. It is their responsibility to tell us what is to be done. They control the educational institutions. They are in charge in the Congress. They sit at the controls of the Federal Reserve System. Power and responsibility cannot be separated.

Hazlitt offered no blueprint in 1946. I offer no blueprint today. I offer only a series of slogans, directed at Keynsians, who do not know what is to be done.

- We told you so.
- We told you why.
- You hold the bag.

The Politics of Plunder.

"Thou shalt not steal."

This is an ethical message. It does not require long chains of reasoning. It does not ask people to follow the money, either backwards or forwards. It just asks them to get their hands out of their neighbors' wallets corporately, by means of state coercion, as well as individually.

There is an aspect of all this that Hazlitt chose to ignore: **bad morals produce bad policies, which in turn produce bad results**. The metaphor of the broken window is a great tool of analysis. But Hazlitt did not focus on this: the state has not adopted its policies of breaking windows because politicians read Keynes' unreadable *General Theory of Employment, Interest, and Money*. The politicians have adopted what Bastiat called the politics of plunder.

Bastiat's broken window metaphor was an extension of his analysis of the politics of plunder in *The Law* (1850). He was not content with providing a superb tool of economic analysis. He also provided the ethical context of the broken window: *theft by the ballot box*. The broken window metaphor allows us to trace the implications of state intervention. But his concept of the politics of plunder gets at the root of the matter: "Thou shalt not steal, except by majority vote."

The masses have demanded that the state use power to redistribute other people's wealth. The masses have voted for politicians who vote for the politics of plunder. The masses have consented to being sheared by the state on this basis: "The rich will be sheared far worse." But the rich hire lawyers and accountants. They avoid the worst of the shearing. They use the politics of plunder to feather their nests at the expense of the masses.

There is ethical cause and effect in life. Morally bad policies produce economically bad results. By placing this fact front and center, my book is different from Hazlitt's. He focused on the broken window. I focus on why the state broke all those windows, and far more—the chapters that Hazlitt did not write, but could have.

The voters have become dependent on the politics of plunder, especially Social Security, which Hazlitt prudently ignored, and above all Medicare, which arrived in 1965. At some point, these welfare programs will bankrupt the federal government.

At some point, Washington's checks will stop coming. That will be the day of reckoning—the day of accounting. That will be the day when the politics of plunder will finally break the windows of those who have voted in terms of this principle: "Thou shalt not steal, except by majority vote."

We are closer to this day of reckoning than Hazlitt was in 1946.

Today, we can get this message out. We have book publishing options with Amazon. We can use free blog sites, such as WordPress.com. We can post free videos on YouTube. We have websites galore to read and write for. This is not 1946.

We do not need to provide a master plan for getting from the politics of plunder to the politics of property protection. The free market will make hash of all such master plans. When Washington's checks stop coming, individuals will respond in terms of the available incentives. Our task is to persuade others not to adopt another round of the politics of plunder locally after the federal government has run out of sheep to shear, as well as funds to break more windows.

Meanwhile, we need to explain to people the implication of these four words: **His. Yours. Mine. Don't.** People do this with their children, but they are severely tempted to forget this when they hear the siren song: "Thou shalt not steal, except by majority vote."

–Appendix–

Henry Hazlitt's Enormous Contribution

It took Hazlitt six weeks to write *Economics in One Lesson* in early 1946. If he devoted 40 hours a week, that would have been about 240 hours. It took me under 100 hours to write my book. I had the advantage of having access to all of his book, and I also had the advantage of 69 years of materials that have been published since the time that he wrote his book. An enormous amount of material has been published.

There are very few, if any, people alive today who read his book when it first came out. It has gained a lot of readers, but initially there were not very many. I don't think there are many people alive today who were part of the libertarian movement in 1946 as a result of either Hazlitt's book or Hayek's *Road to Serfdom* (1944). Therefore, people do not appreciate the remarkable nature of Hazlitt's efforts in 1946.

He could not refer to a developed body of materials on the topics he covered in his book. There was no such body of materials. Today, we have more than we can possibly read.

Today, we are the beneficiaries of the World Wide Web. This includes PDF's, websites, YouTube, Amazon, Facebook, Wordpress.com, and all of the other tools of communication. It is extraordinary what has taken place since 1999. I first went online with my site in 1996, and the change since then has been mind-boggling.

We are told that Hazlitt's book has sold something in the range of 700,000 copies. This means about 10,000 copies a year for almost 70 years. Yet I will mail out the final chapter of my book to something in the range of 90,000 people. That will cost me a few dollars. The technology today enables people to communicate ideas on a scale never imagined by Hazlitt or anybody else in 1946.

When he wrote his book, he was almost alone. Hayek and Ludwig von Mises were in the United States, but Mises was virtually unknown. In the same year that Hazlitt wrote his book, Leonard Read started the Foundation for Economic Education, which was a tiny operation. There were no Washington Beltway think tanks that promoted free-market ideas.

Communications among libertarians barely existed. For that matter, there really wasn't anything known as libertarianism. Conservatives in 1946 were mainly besieged holdouts of the late 1930s political opposition of Franklin Roosevelt,[1] but there was no developed conservative philosophy. There was no conservative magazine. The Saturday Evening Post did occasionally publish articles by free market advocates, but there was nothing ideological about that magazine.

In 1946, a conservative could hardly find materials to read. Today, he could not possibly read in a year more than a tiny fraction of the materials that are published every day on the Web.

In 1955, William F. Buckley started National Review. The next year, the Foundation for Economic Education began publishing The Freeman. Up until that time, there was almost nothing to read. Reading materials were limited to newsletters, and only a handful of people had ever heard of any of these newsletters. You don't know what the blackout was like in 1955, unless you were there, and those of us who were there don't remember 1946.

In January 1946, the only free market book that non-economists had heard of was Hayek's Road to Serfdom. That was because the Reader's Digest published a précis of it in 1945. You can read that précis online.[2]

---

1. http://www.intercollegiatereview.com/index.php/2015/06/17/conservative-hero-josiah-bailey/

2. http://www.garynorth.com/HayekRoadRD.pdf

The good old days were bad. If we are talking about materials that could be used to defend the free market, 1946 was a wasteland. Hazlitt's book was an oasis in the midst of the Gobi desert.

Keynesians still dominate the mainstream media and the universities, but they no longer get a free ride. When the day of fiscal reckoning comes, the vultures will be circling overhead. They are going to pick clean the corpse of Keynesianism.

If we are talking about home-grown American authors, Henry Hazlitt deserves credit as the most important defender of the free market in the 1940's. He stood alone in his day. That took courage. That took intelligence. It was a good thing that he was one of the best writers in the financial media. *Newsweek* was smart enough to hire him after *The New York Times* was dumb enough to fire him.

What I remember most about him in the early 1970's was his laughter. In this respect, he was a lot like Murray Rothbard. He had been in the trenches for four decades by the time I met him. The experience had not ground him down.

He never stopped learning. He was always reading. He never stopped writing, either. If he had something to say, he said it in print. *The Freeman* was always open to him.[3]

---

3. For a list of his publications in *The Freeman*, see http://fee.org/people/henry-hazlitt.